World's Greatest
WRITERS

Wonder House

(An imprint of Prakash Books)

Wonder House
(An imprint of Prakash Books)

contact@wonderhousebooks.com

© Wonder House Books 2023

ISBN : 9789388369039

CONTENTS

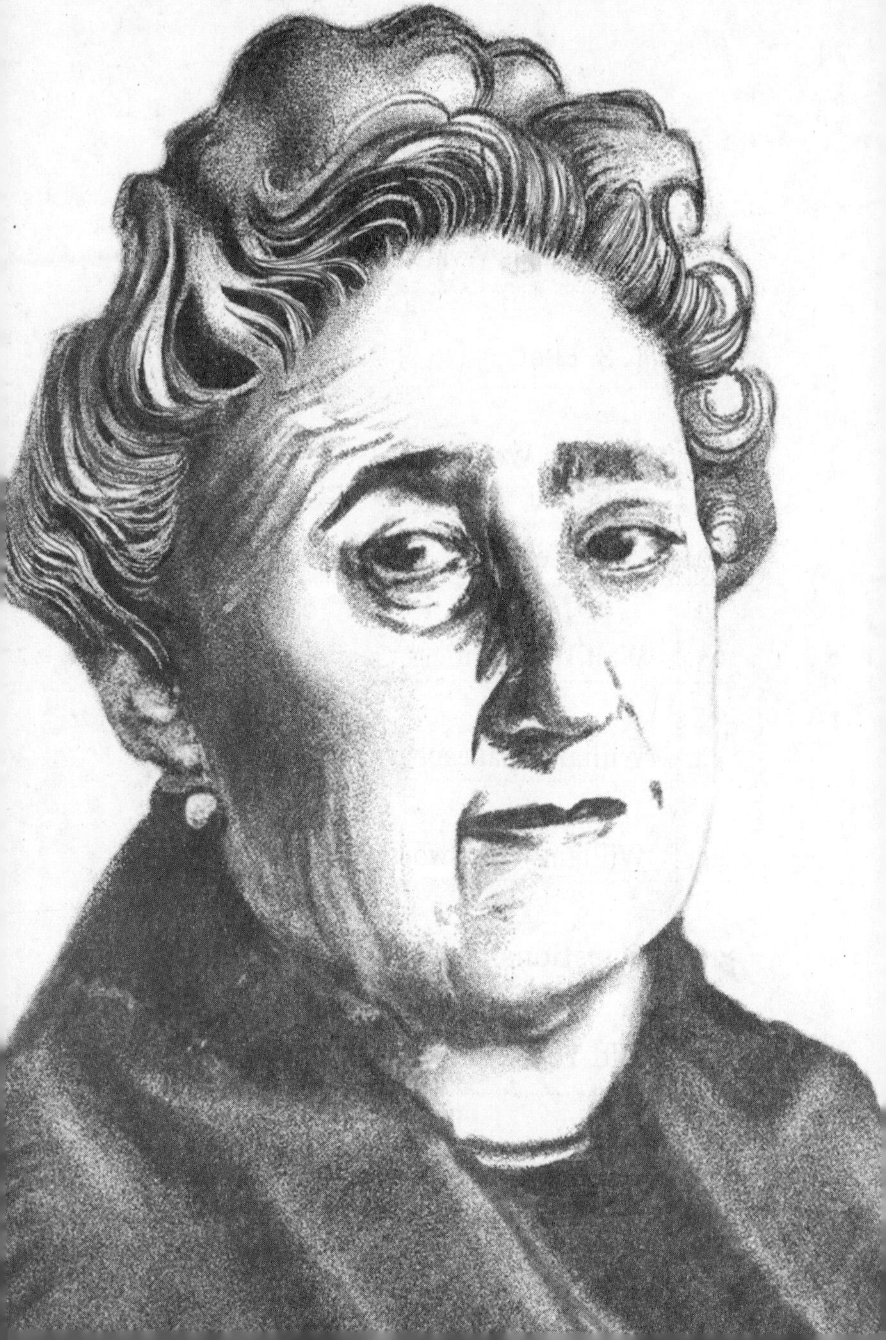

AGATHA CHRISTIE

BIRTH: *September 15, 1890*
Torquay, England

DEATH: *January 12, 1976 (aged 85)*
Wallingford, England

Agatha Christie was an English detective novelist and playwright. She wrote over 66 detective novels and 14 short story collections. Her best work includes *Murder on the Orient Express* and *The Mystery of the Blue Train*. She was known as the 'Queen of Crime'. She wrote *The Mousetrap,* the play with the longest continuous run at a theater.

Agatha Mary Clarissa Christie was born on September 15, 1890 in Torquay, England to Frederick Alvah Miller and Clarissa Boehmer Miller. She was the youngest of three children. Her father was an American stockbroker and her mother was a storyteller. She was home-schooled by her mother. Her parents didn't want her to learn to read until the age of eight. Alone at home, Agatha, taught herself to read by the age of five. In 1901, her father passed away which led her family into a financial crisis. Her mother inspired her to write poetry and short stories. Young Agatha was interested in writing poems. Her work was even published in *The Poetry Review*.

She started her literary career by writing short stories. Her first story was *The House of Beauty* (later *The House of Dreams*). The story described the world of madness and dreams. She used mysticism as a central element in most of her stories. She also wrote a novel called *Snow Upon the Desert*. However, the novel was never published. During World War I, she volunteered and nursed soldiers at the hospital in Torquay, England.

Later, she started to work on her detective novel *The Mysterious Affair of Styles*. The book got published in

1920. In her crime novels, she used several real-life experiences and factual information. For instance, during World War I she learned about various poisons when she worked in the hospital. She was praised for her well-described scenes involving poison in the story. It was also published in the famous *Pharmaceutical Journal*. In 1922, her second novel, *The Secret Adversary* was released and the third novel, *Murder on the Links* came out in 1923.

She was as famous for her plays, as she was for fiction. She released works like *The Hollow* (1951) and *Verdict* (1958). Her play titled *The Mousetrap* held a record for the longest-running show in London's Ambassadors Theatre. The play opened in 1952 and it ran for more than 8862 performances. Many of Christie's stories were made into famous movies like *Murder on the Orient Express* and *Death on the Nile*. Her last public appearance was on the opening night of her play *Murder on the Orient Express* in 1974.

Agatha married Archibald Christie on Christmas Eve in 1914 and had a daughter, Roseline. Their marriage didn't last and she divorced him in 1928. The second time she married archeologist Max Mallowan. Her experiences of traveling with Mallowan in the Middle East provided a background for several of her detective novels. She described her trips in *Come, Tell Me How You Live*, an autobiographical and travel piece, and in *The Murder at the Vicarage*.

Agatha's most famous characters were "Poirot" and "Marple", which she used in many of her novels and short stories. New York Times published an obituary when Agatha killed Poirot in 1975's *Curtains*. She later revealed that her character, Miss Marple, who appeared in twelve novels and five short story collections, was influenced by her grandmother.

Agatha's significant works include the novel *Murder in Mesopotamia* published in 1936. The characters that she used in this book are based on archeologists that she met in real life. In 1938, the book *Appointment with Death* came out. The places that she mentioned in her novel were personally explored by Christie and then written about in the book.

Given her success as an author, she was known as the 'Queen of Mystery' and the 'Queen of Crime.' She became the top-selling author of all time. Billions of copies of all her works were sold worldwide. She wrote around eighty novels during her active years. Many of her books were adapted into films, television shows and even video games. Christie died in 1976, at the age of 85.

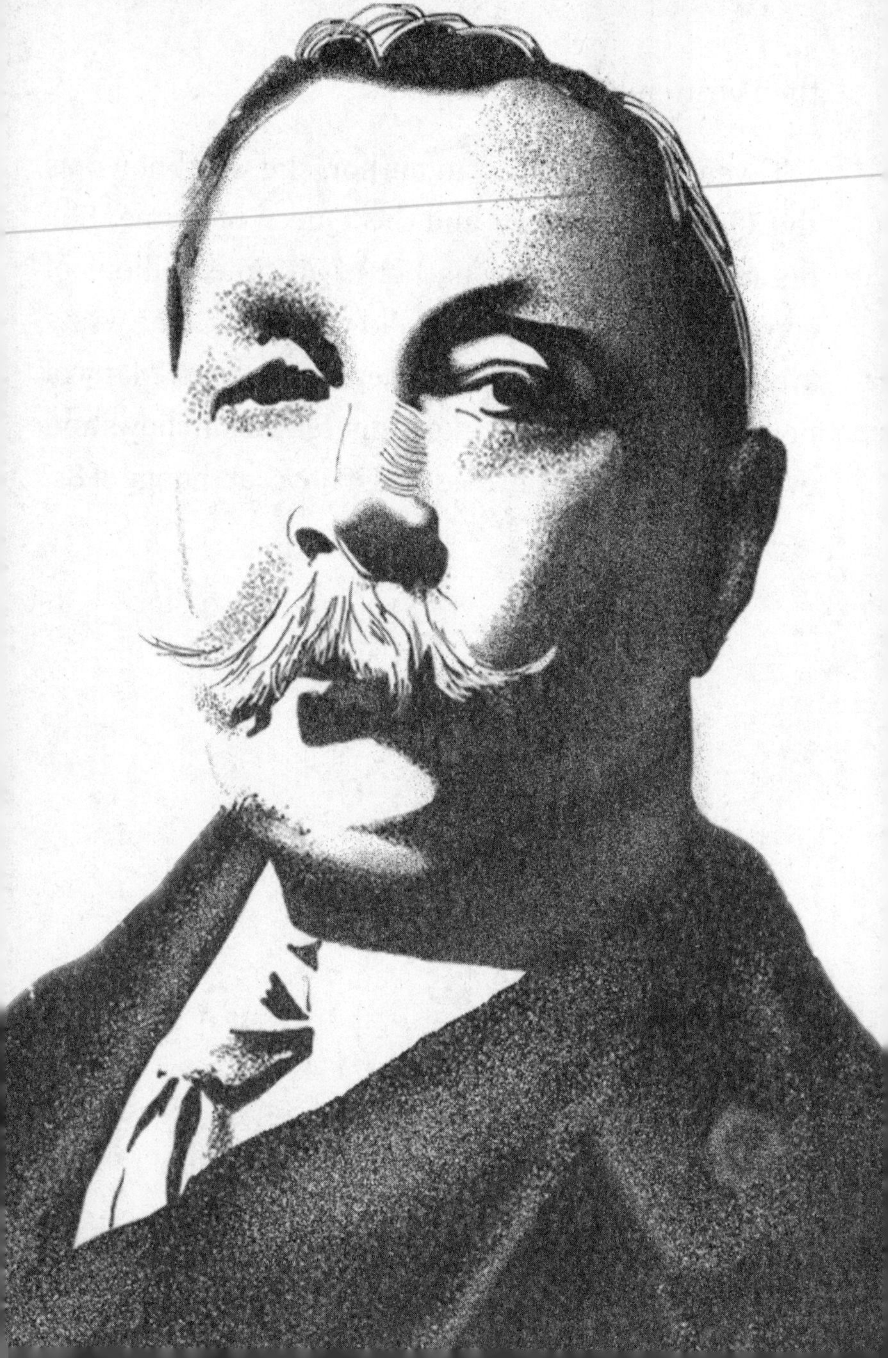

ARTHUR CONAN DOYLE

BIRTH: *May 22, 1859*
Edinburgh, Scotland

DEATH: *July 7, 1930 (aged 71)*
Crowborough, England

Arthur Conan Doyle was a Scottish author. He created one of the most famous fictional characters in English detective fiction, Sherlock Holmes.

Sir Arthur Ignatius Conan Doyle was born on May 22, 1859 in Edinburgh, Scotland, to Charles Altamont Doyle and Mary Foley. His father was an artist and his mother was a storyteller. It was his mother who inspired young Arthur to take an interest in history and literature. Arthur wrote his first story about a Bengal tiger and a hunter at the age of five.

For his education, he went to a Jesuit boarding school, and later attended the Stonyhurst College. He worked on a student paper called Feldkirch Gazette. Arthur's uncle, who was a famous journalist, also inspired him to write. Arthur was an avid reader. Edgar Allan Poe's works greatly influenced his detective fiction.

In 1876, he attended the University of Edin-burgh and studied medicine. His writing career also started during this time. *The Haunted Grange of Goresthorpe* is one of his earliest works of fiction, from the 1870s.

Doyle first began writing short stories. In 1879, his first publication, *The Mystery of Sasassa Valley*, was published in the *Chambers' Journal*. During his time as a medical student, he went on a sea voyage to the Arctic. On the journey, Doyle wrote a fascinating story called *The Captain of the Pole Star*.

He wrote short stories for the *London Society*, *All the Year Round*, *Temple Bar*, *Lancet* and *The Strand Magazine*. He began to write his first novel, The Narrative of John Smith, during this time. It was written in 1883 but was published much after his death, in 2011, by the British Library.

In 1887, *A Study in Scarlet* was published in the *Beeton's Christmas Annual*. It received good reviews and introduced the celebrated characters of Sherlock Holmes and Dr John Watson. Next, Doyle considered writing historical romances. He came up with his first historical novel, *Micah Clarke* in 1889. His novel *The Mystery of Cloomber* was also published in 1888 and *The Firm of Girdlestone* was published in 1890. The book was later made into a silent film. That year, he published his second Sherlock Holmes novel, *The Sign of the Four*. The next year, he came up with *The Adventures of Sherlock Holmes* series. It consisted of twelve stories where he re-introduced his famous detective character.

The Parasite and *The Memoirs of Sherlock Holmes* were released between 1893-1895. The character of Sherlock Holmes dies in the latter. In 1893, Doyle co-authored the comic opera *Jane Annie* or *The Good Conduct Prize*. With his detective novels' success, he became quite well-known all around the world. Doyle used his popular fictional character Sherlock Holmes in more than fifty detective stories. He was amongst the first to explore the mystery genre.

He also released his poetry collection *The Guards Came Through and Other Poems* in 1919, and some non-fiction works like *The Coming of the Fairies, The Case for Spirit Photography*, etc.

He wrote short stories in many genres including horror, suspense, psychological thriller and science fiction. His second most famous character was Professor George Edward Challenger. He was first introduced in the *Professor Challenger* stories in 1912. This series contained science fiction stories. Doyle's body of literary works is enormous. He wrote many novels and hundreds of short stories in his lifetime.

Arthur married twice and had five children. He died at the age of 71, on July 7, 1930, in England, due to a heart attack.

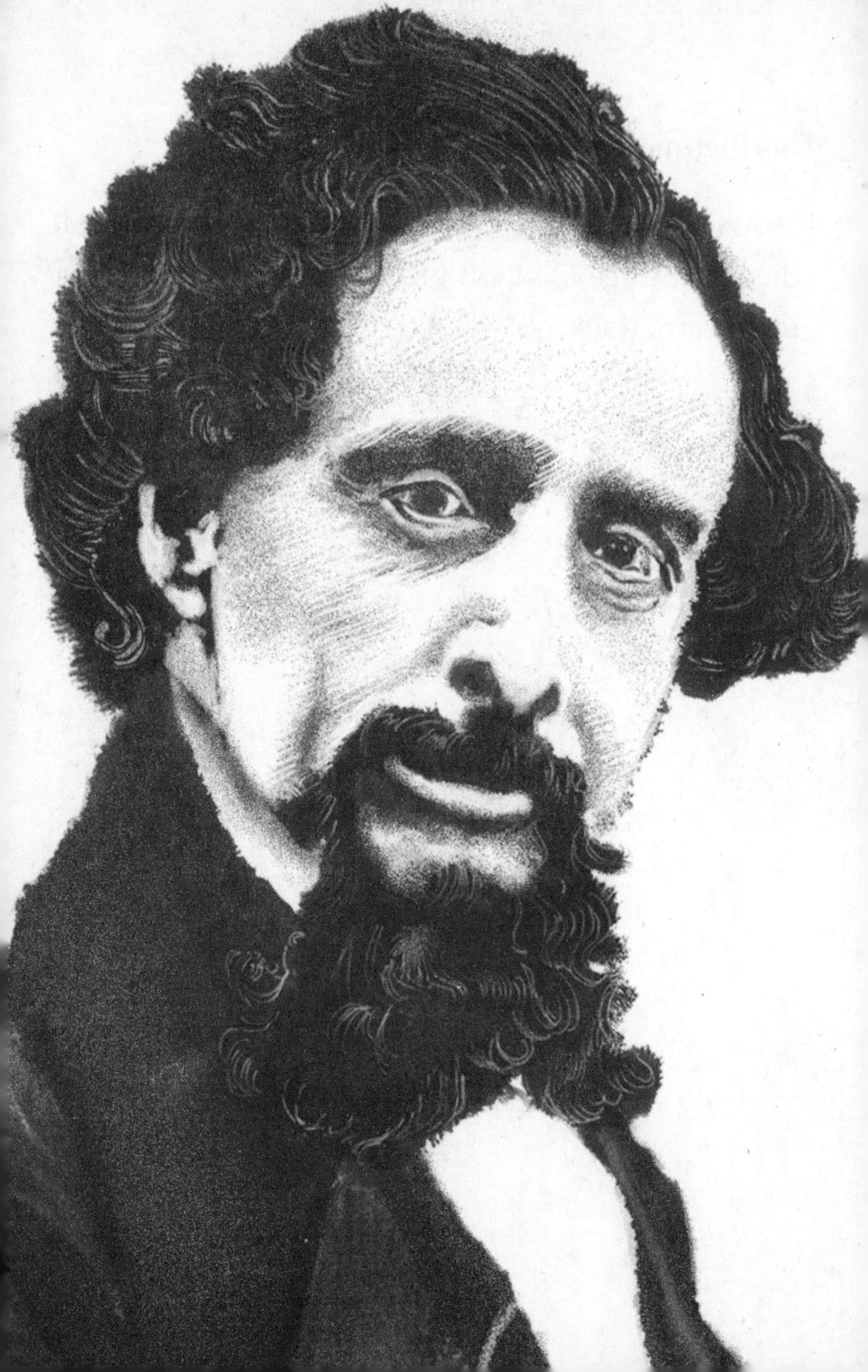

CHARLES DICKENS

BIRTH: *February 7, 1812*
Portsmouth, England

DEATH: *June 9, 1870 (aged 58)*
Chatham, England

Charles Dickens is one of the most famous authors in the history of literature. His books were based on hard-hitting themes like poverty, child labor and slavery. Dickens drew heavily from his own life for his writing. His best works include *Oliver Twist, A Christmas Carol* and *Hard Times*.

Charles John Huffam Dickens was born in Portsmouth, England on February 7, 1812, to John and Elizabeth Dickens. His father worked as a clerk in the pay office of the Royal Dockyard. Dickens had a tough childhood and his family struggled financially. Forced by poverty, they moved to Camden Town, a poor neighborhood of London, in 1822. His experiences there inspired much of his adult work.

Dickens' father was imprisoned for debt when he was only twelve years old, and he was forced to work in a shoe polish factory to support his family. It had a profound psychological impact on him. His experiences with poverty left him with the most influential voice of the working class in his era. He went back to school for his final two years of education and graduated at the age of fifteen.

Dickens found a job as an office boy. During the 1830s, he worked as a shorthand court reporter and a newspaper reporter. These experiences became a stepping stone for Dickens' writing career. He became a parliamentary reporter in 1831. In 1833, he started to write short stories and essays for various publications. Dickens published his first story *A Dinner at Poplar Walk*, which also appeared in the *Monthly Magazine* in 1833. Dickens continued his reporting career and joined *The Morning Chronicle*. His connections to these different magazines and newspapers helped him publish many fiction books.

One of his famous works from the time was *The Pickwick Papers of the Pickwick Club*. It was published monthly, till 1837. *The Pickwick Papers* was a great success. He furthered his literary career and became the editor of a monthly magazine, *Bentley's Miscellany*. He produced many works in a short period, like *Oliver Twist* in 1837, and *Nicholas Nickleby* in 1839. *The Old Curiosity Shop* was written as part of the *Master Humphrey's Clock* series in 1840 and *Barnaby Rudge* came out in 1841. Before he released his works as books, he published them in monthly installments.

In 1842, he went to the United States. There, he wrote his controversial piece, *American Notes*.

During 1843-49, Dickens published three

stories. The books were *A Christmas Carol, The Chimes* and *The Cricket on the Hearth*. Out of these three, *A Christmas Carol* became an instant best-seller. The book has amongst the highest number of movie adaptations. He continued to publish novels like *Dombey and Son* and *The Life of Our Lord*.

In 1850, Dickens worked as an editor for the weekly periodical, *Household Words*. He released novels like *Bleak House, Hard Times, Little Dorrit* and *A Tale of Two Cities* between 1851-59. These novels were very successful and more people started appreciating his writing style.

In 1865, he got into an accident while traveling in England. Around the same time, he wrote a short story called *The Signal-Man*. His last few works include his wildly popular novel, and Dickens' personal "favorite child", *David Copperfield*. The book was seen as a semi-autobiography of Dickens', with characters inspired by his parents. He seems to have narrated the struggle of his life in the book, from working in a shoe factory and going on to become a reporter.

In 1836, he married Catherine Hogarth, daughter of the editor of the *Evening Chronicle*. The couple had ten children before they got separated in 1858. In 1870, he suffered from paralysis. He remained unconscious and died on 9th June, 1870, at the age of 58, in England.

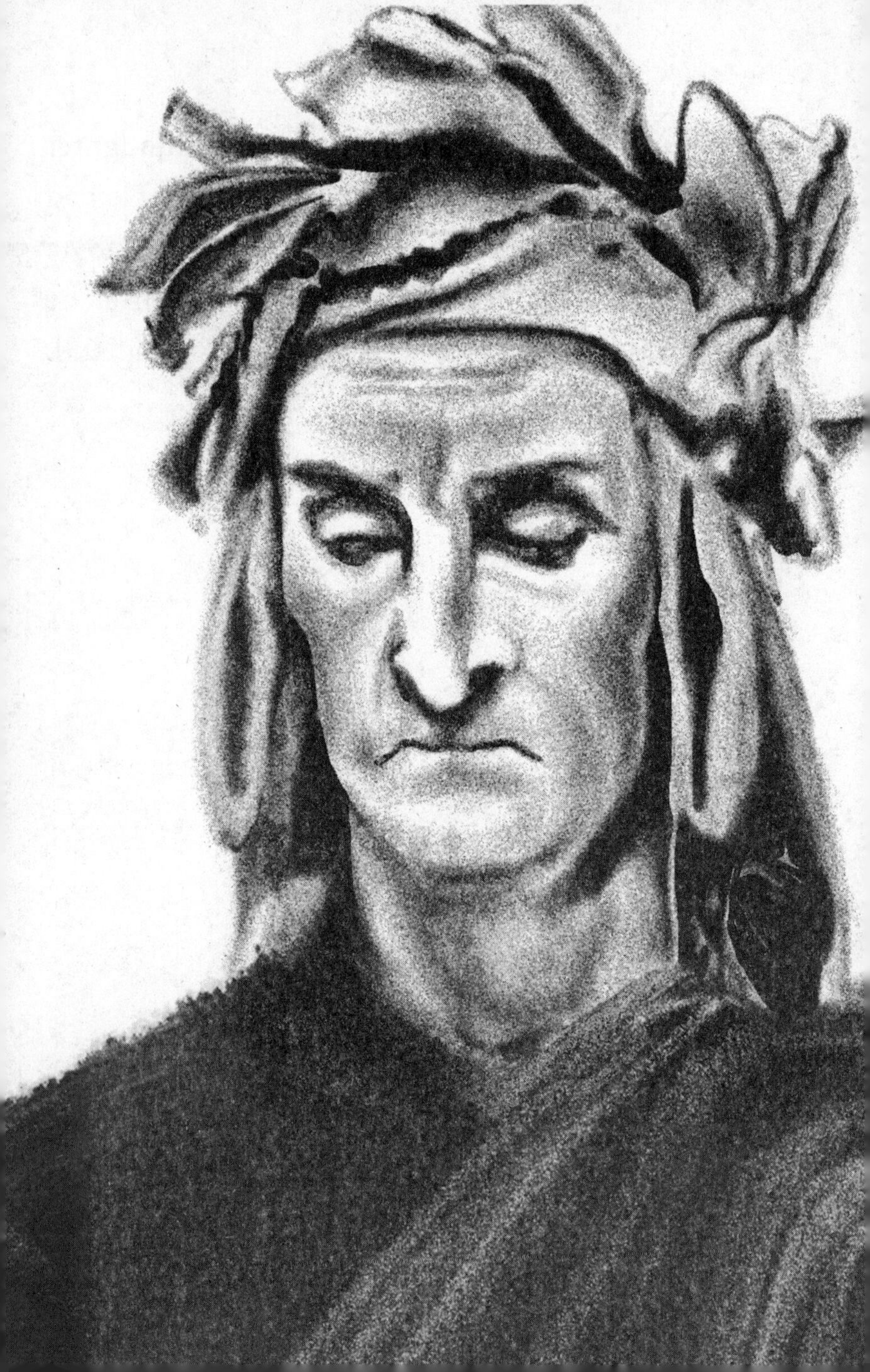

DANTE ALIGHIERI

BIRTH: *1265, Florence, Italy*

DEATH: *September 1321*
Ravenna, Italy

Dante Alighieri was an Italian poet, prose writer, literary theorist, philosopher and political thinker. Dante is referred to as the 'Father of the Italian Language'.

Dante Alighieri was born in 1265 in Florence, Italy to Alighiero di Bellincione and Donna Bella Abati. He studied many subjects like Tuscan poetry, painting and music.

When he lost his father, the poet Brunetto Latini

became Dante's guardian and mentor. Dante was heavily influenced by his work. Dante was at the helm of a new literary style called Dolce Stil Novo (or sweet new style). The idea behind joining the movement was to celebrate an idealized view of love and womanhood. He started writing professionally in 1283. His first work was called *The New Life*. He wrote it in Italian. The book took him many years to complete and was finally published in 1295.

Dante soon fell in love with Beatrice Portinari. She became a muse for Dante's most famous work, *The Divine Comedy*.

Dante was also very involved in politics. As a politician, he achieved very little success, but he held various positions in the city over the years.

In 1302, Dante was exiled from Florence by the Black Guelphs, the faction in power at the time. Dante traveled a lot during his exile. While traveling, he wrote many works including *The Divine Comedy*, one of the most significant literary narratives produced in the medieval period. It was based on Dante's own experience of exile. A three-part poem, it is divided into Inferno, Purgatorio and Paradiso. By the time he finished *The Divine Comedy*, it consisted of more than 14,233 lines. The legendary poem contains a story about a fictional journey through hell, purification, and paradise, and the journey of the soul towards God. The poem made waves and was revolutionary in its own way, and even changed the fate of Italian in Europe. Thus, Dante influenced the course of literary development. He also wrote *The Eloquent Vernacular* between 1302-1305.

Both these books helped establish Italian as an important literary language. He argued that the vernacular ought to be given the same respect and importance as the Latin language. This book became influential even before it was published.

Having already had an interest in philosophy, he then also wrote some of his most important works in the field.

Dante lived in Bologna for a few years, until Florentine exiles were banished and he moved on to Padua. When Dante wrote against the Florence government, he was exiled from Florence permanently.

In 1315, the government insisted that ex- patriots were required to pay a heavy fine and had to go through public punishment. Dante remained in exile and refused to pay a fine. It was politics that got him into trouble and led him to his exile from his own country. Dante worked as a member of the White Guelph, who were moderates. The Black Guelphs accused Dante of crimes he had not committed. However, Dante never showed up to defend himself. So, it was ordered that he be burnt at the stake, but this never materialized.

An arrangement was made when Dante was around twelve years old that he would marry Gemma Donati, the daughter of a family friend. They got married in 1285 and had four children. But, Dante had been in love with another woman called Beatrice Portinari for years. She had a significant influence on Dante's works.

He died at the age of 56, in 1321, in Venice, most likely of malaria. Dante left behind a great legacy and was known as an excellent writer who created his best works while in exile.

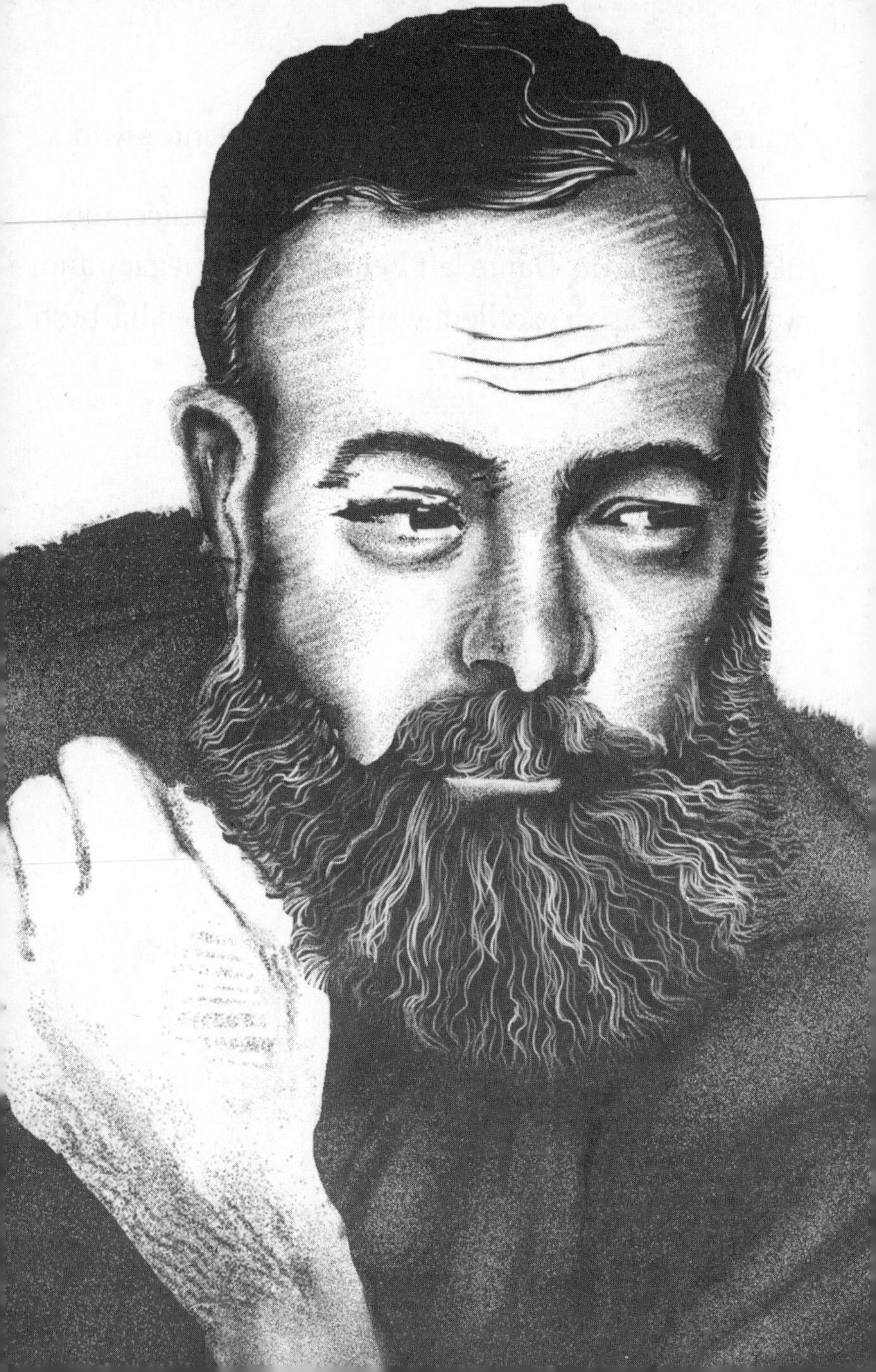

ERNEST HEMINGWAY

BIRTH: July 21, 1899
Oak Park, Illinois, USA

DEATH: July 2, 1961 (aged 61)
Ketchum, Idaho, USA

Ernest Miller Hemingway was an American novelist and short story writer. He was awarded the Nobel Prize for Literature in 1954.

Ernest Miller Hemingway was born on July 21, 1899 at Oak Park, Illinois, Chicago to Dr Clarence and Grace Hemingway. From a young age, Ernest shared his father's interests. He would observe nature and lived outdoors for camping, fishing and hiking. All these experiences later reflected in Hemingway's stories such as *The Nick Adams Stories* and the famous *The Old Man and the Sea*.

Ernest attended Oak Park School and then River Forest High School. In 1915, he wrote for his high school newspaper and literary magazine. After he graduated in 1917 from Oak Park High School, he accepted a job as a reporter for *The Kansas City Star*. He also wrote for *Star Weekly* and *Toronto Star*. His career in journalism significantly impacted his literary style.

In 1918, Hemingway wanted to join the military, but he was rejected because of his weak left eye. So, he decided to do voluntary work instead. He went to Italy with the American Red Cross.

While in Italy, he got severely wounded by a cannon. In his famous war novel, *A Farewell to Arms* he shared his experiences of World War I with the readers. Hemingway returned to the United States in 1919, after he was discharged from the Red Cross. Later, he was hired as a correspondent at the *Toronto Star*.

His first book, *Three Stories & Ten Poems* was

published by Contact Publishing in 1923. He started to work on his next project called *In Our Time*, a collection of short stories published in 1925.

In 1926, he published his first major novel called *The Sun Also Rises*. The characters of the book belong to the Lost Generation, the people who came of age around World War I, predictably affected by the war. Hemingway himself belonged to this generation. Later, he released many works like *The Torrents of Spring* and *Today is Friday*. He signed a contract with Scribner Publishing in 1926, and published with them.

He wrote *A Farewell to Arms* in 1929. It was a poignant tale of love and war during World War I. Hemingway went on a safari in Africa in 1934, which gave him new ideas for his next books. The novels *The Green Hills of Africa* and *Snows of Kilimanjaro* were based on accounts of his safari adventures. These books were published in 1935 and 1936 respectively.

Hemingway served as a war reporter during the Spanish Civil War. He funded the Loyalist cause and published *To Have and Have Not* in 1937. It was a best-selling political novel. The next year, he published *The Fifth Column and the First Forty-Nine Stories,* set in the backdrop of the Great Depression. In 1940, he released *For Whom the Bell Tolls,* another one of his hit novels.

In 1944, he covered World War II and became a correspondent for *Collier's.* He published *Across the River and Into the Trees* in 1950. The novel was based on a romance set in post-war Europe. It was well-received near the end of the 20th century.

In 1951, Hemingway wrote *The Old Man and the Sea,* which became his most appreciated work. He won the Pulitzer Prize for this in 1953.

Ernest Hemingway married four times. He was the father of three children. In his later years, Hemingway bought a home in Ketchum, Idaho in 1959. There, he wrote *A Moveable Feast,* a memoir about his years in Paris. He died on July 2, 1961, at the age of 61, in Idaho.

A few of Hemingway's works were published

posthumously. *Islands in the Stream* and *The Dangerous Summer* were published in 1970 and 1985 respectively. Hemingway's works remain a valuable contribution to twentieth-century literature and continue to inspire future generations.

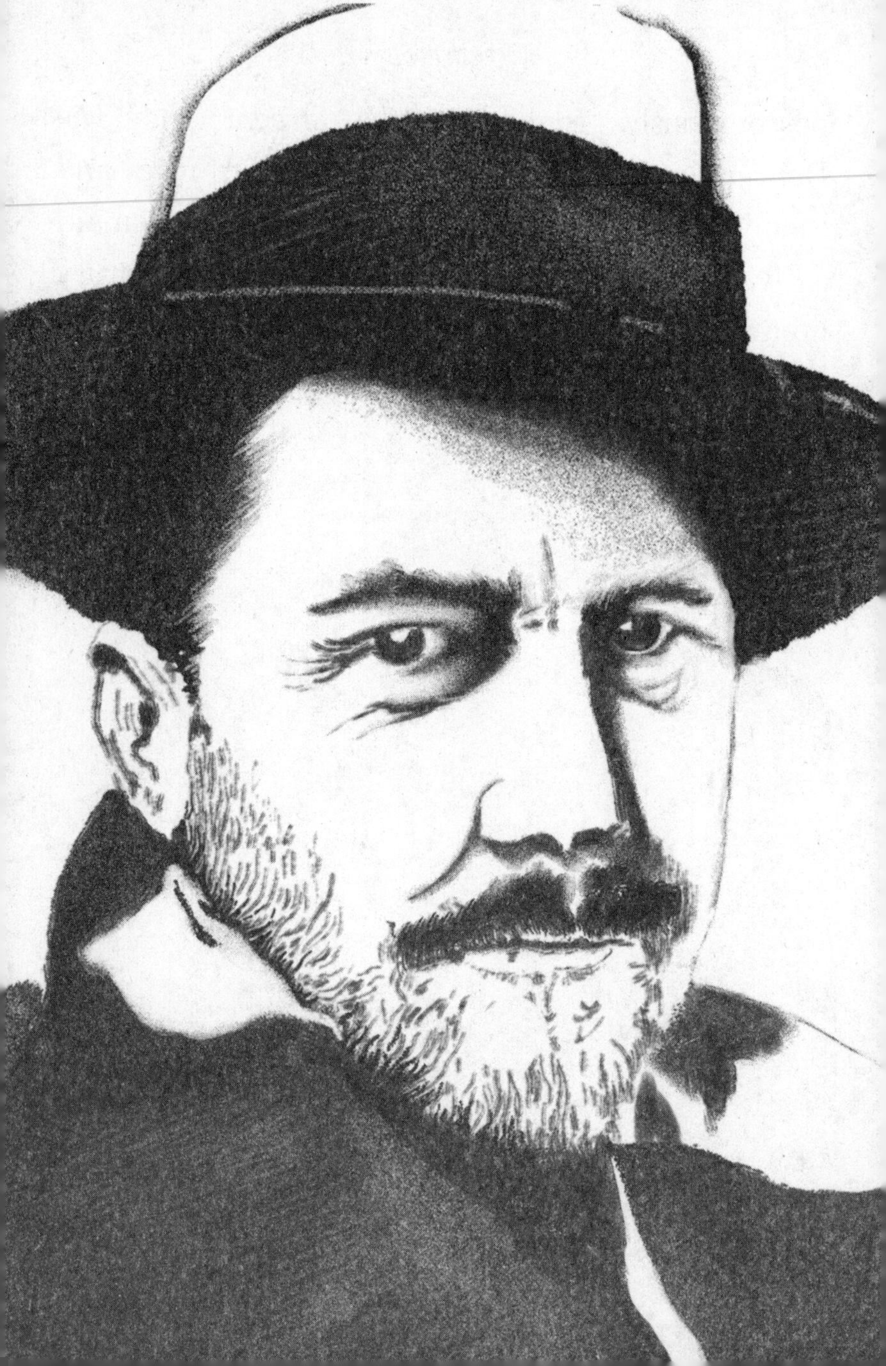

EZRA POUND

BIRTH: *October 30, 1885*
Hailey, Idaho, USA

DEATH: *November 1, 1972 (aged 87)*
Venice, Italy

Ezra Pound was an American poet, critic and intellectual, who was a significant figure in the Modernist movement in early to mid-twentieth century poetry.

Ezra Loomis Pound was born on 30th October, 1885 in the small mining town of Hailey, Idaho to Homer and Isabel Pound. When he was only eighteen months old, his family moved to Philadelphia, where his father became an official at the United States Mint. In 1897, Ezra attended Cheltenham Military Academy, which he left after two years, without graduating. Later, he went to a local high school. He had a knowledge of Latin, English, History, Arithmetic and French.

At the age of eleven, he published a humorous five-line poem; it was his first. After he graduated from school, he enrolled at University of Pennsylvania's College of Liberal Arts, but transferred to Hamilton College, New York, after two years, to get a bachelor's degree in philosophy. He returned to the University of Pennsylvania and earned an MA in Romance languages in 1906.

In 1908, he published his very first books, *A Lume Spento,* and *A Quinzaine for this Yule* with his own money. He convinced Elkin Mathews, a London publisher and bookseller, to promote these. Mathews helped Pound and published his next three books.

The first book out of the three was *Personae of Ezra Pound*, published in 1909. The other two books were *Exultations of Ezra Pound* and *The Spirit of Romance*. In 1911, he wrote a weekly column for *The New Age journal*. He also started to teach at Regent Street

Polytechnic.

Pound gave birth to a movement called Imagism in the early 1920s. It aimed at replacing useless words, instead favoring sharp and precise language in poetry. He wanted poets to write such that their writing described the object exactly, and served as verbal images. In 1912, Pound began to work as a journalist for *Poetry*, a Chicago-based magazine. For the job, he reviewed the works of upcoming poets like Robert Frost and D. H. Lawrence. His next work was *Ripostes of Ezra Pound* in 1912. The book contained 25 poems. It was the first example of Imagism.

Pound also started working on *The Cantos* during this time. In 1917, he released the first section of this ambitious project. Ezra completed his 18-part work *Hugh Selwy Writers Mauberley* (1921). In 1924, he moved to Italy and turned his full attention towards finishing *The Cantos. A Draft of XVI Cantos* was published in 1925. Later, other editions were released including *Eleven New Cantos, 1934; The*

Fifth Decade of Cantos, 1937; *Cantos LII-LXXI*, 1940.

Despite Pound working on *The Cantos* from 1915 to 1962, the project remained incomplete. It contained 116 sections and each section was referred to as one canto. These poems were based on different themes like economics, governance, culture and more. It was a mix of satire, chants and essays.

Ezra was also interested in politics and did not return to the United States until 1945. The same year he was arrested for broadcasting fascist propaganda by radio during World War II. He was declared mentally unstable on the plea of his lawyers and sent to St Elizabeth's Hospital in Washington, D.C. In April 1958, Pound was set free. During his time in the hospital, he was allowed to read and write. So, he completed his poems *Section: Rock-Drill* in 1955 and *Thrones* in 1959; both were a part of *The Cantos*.

Pound married Dorothy Shakespear on 20th April, 1914, while he was in London. They had one son, Omar, who was raised by Dorothy's mother, Olivia

Shakespear. He also had an affair with the American violinist Olga Rudge with whom he had a daughter named Mary. Olga took care of Pound during the last eleven years of his life.

He died in Venice, Italy, on November 1, 1972. Throughout his life Pound published seventy books and authored more than thousands of articles. He was recognized for his literary prowess and was awarded the Bollingen Prize for Poetry for the same.

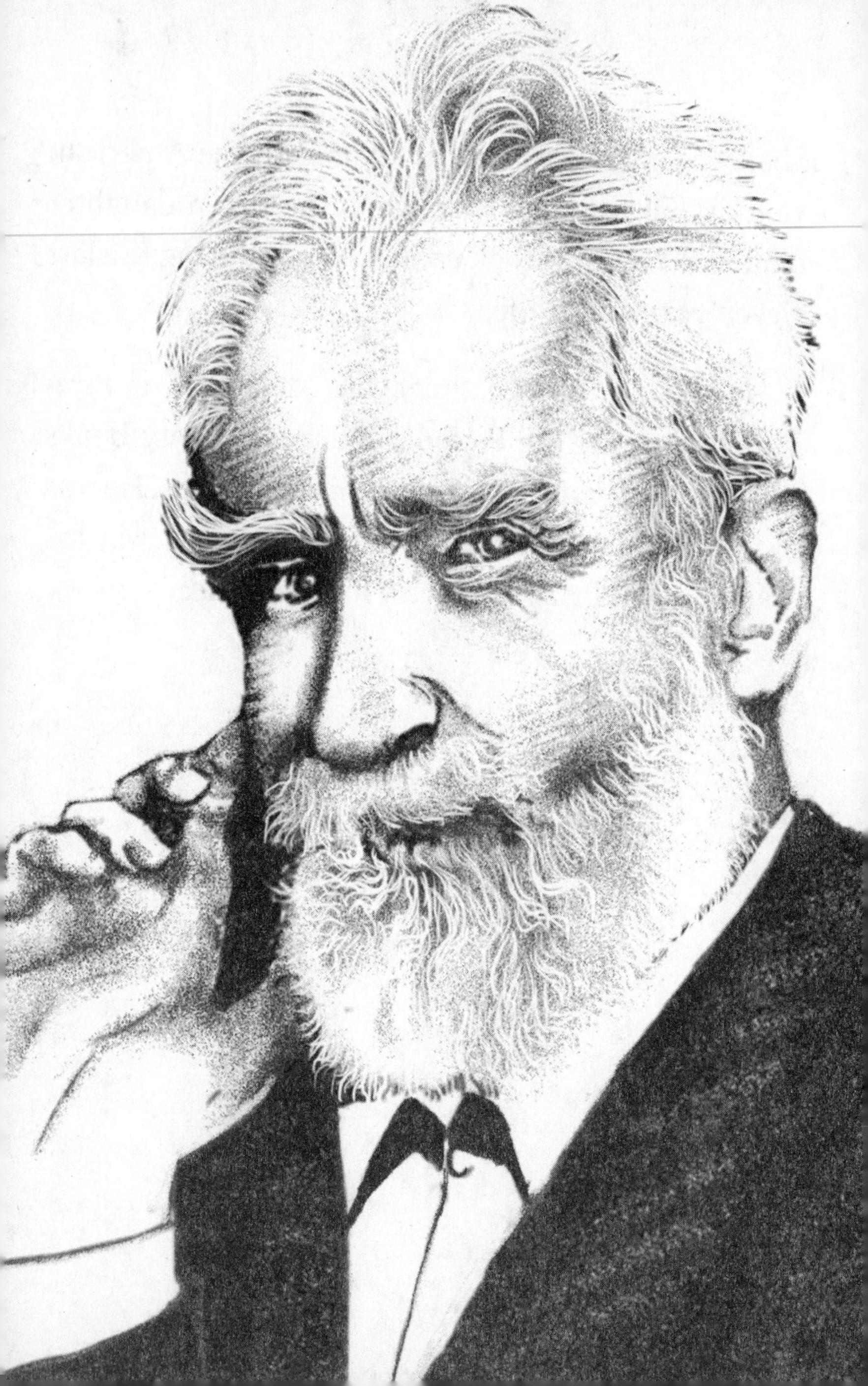

GEORGE BERNARD SHAW

BIRTH: July 26, 1856
Dublin, Ireland

DEATH: November 2, 1950 (aged 94)
Hertfordshire, England

George Bernard Shaw was a Nobel-winning Irish playwright and literary critic. His most notable works include *Pygmalion, My Fair Lady* and *Arms and the Man.*

George Bernard Shaw was born on July 26, 1856 in Dublin, Ireland, to George Carr Shaw and Lucinda Elizabeth Shaw. He was tutored by his uncle before he attended the Wesley College in Dublin. Then, he was transferred to a private school. Later, he continued his studies at the Central Model School in Dublin.

George gained knowledge about art, music and literature from his visits to the National Gallery of Ireland and through his mother. By the age of sixteen, he started to work in an agency and traveled to London. He struggled financially. It was there that he worked on his first novel. Shaw's semi-autobiographical work, *Immaturity*, written in 1879 but published in 1930, failed to garner any interest. His next four novels, along with most of the articles he submitted to the press, were rejected as well.

He started to take an interest in politics. Shaw was an activist and a socialist. He joined the Fabian Society, a non-revolutionary group that sought to spread socialism through permeation. He edited articles for *Fabian Essays in Socialism* in 1889. He was selected by Frank Harris and became a theatre critic for the *Saturday Review*. Consequently, he started to write plays on serious themes.

Shaw became a staff journalist for the *Pall Mall Gazette* in 1885. Later, he published his plays in a book called *Pleasant and Unpleasant*. His works *Arms and the Man*, *Candida* and *You Never Can Tell* were considered in *Pleasant*, while *Widower's Houses*, *The Philanderer* and *Mrs Warren's Profession* were a part of *Unpleasant*.

Shaw's *Arms and the Man* was published in 1894. It was a satire on the romanticized and popular ideas of war. He then came up with his next book, *Mrs Warren's Profession*. The story shed light on the economic conditions and struggles that led women to questionable professions. Shaw never took a break from his writing.

In 1895, he released *Candida*. It was admired for its powerful character portrayals. The plot revolved around Candida's marriage, questioning the Victorian ideals of love, marriage, and a woman's true desires. In 1904, *Candida* was successfully performed at the Royal Court Theatre in London.

In 1901, *Three Plays for Puritans* was pub- lished, which included *The Devil's Disciple,* a Victorian melodrama set during the American Revolution. The play was an instant success. Shaw went on to write *Caesar* and *Cleopatra* and *The Admirable Bashville,* which were two of his most brilliant plays of all time.

In his later years as a writer, Shaw's remarkable works included *Saint Joan* and *John Bull's Other Island.* Shaw established himself as a leading dramatist of his time, especially after he won the Nobel Prize for Literature in 1925.

Shaw's 1913 hit *Pygmalion* was perhaps his most famous commercial success and certainly his most humorous work. It was also adapted into a film that released in 1938 and was later adapted into a Broadway musical named *My Fair Lady* in 1956. The movie version of *Pygmalion* received an Oscar for the best screenplay in 1938.

Shaw lived a happy married life with Charlotte Payn,

whom he married in 1898. She was also a part of the Fabian Society.

He died at the age of 94 on November 2, 1950.

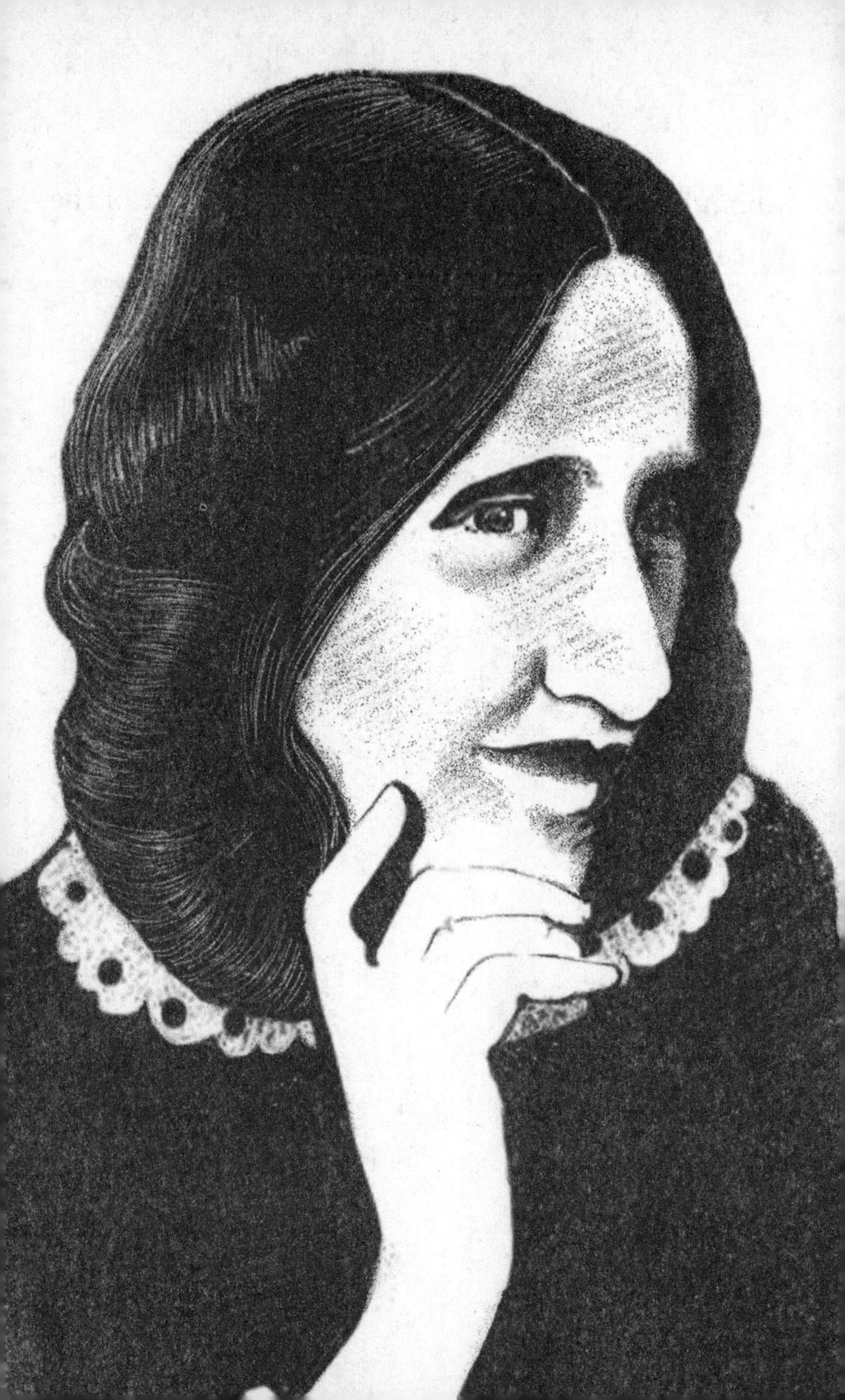

GEORGE ELIOT

BIRTH: November 22, 1819
Chilvers Coton, England

DEATH: December 22, 1880 (aged 61)
London, England

George Eliot was an English novelist, poet, and translator. One of her major works was *Middlemarch*, which is recognized as one of the most significant books in the history of English fiction.

George Eliot was the pen name for Mary Ann Evans. She was born on 22nd November, 1819 in Chilvers Coton, England to Robert Evans and Christiana Pearson. She had a warm and comfortable home. The fields and hedgerows of her native country provided the setting of many of her novels, like *Silas Marner*. Her education revolved around Christian teachings and agreed with the traditions of the day.

Eliot found her passion for reading and writing during her time at a boarding school, where she learned French and Italian. In 1837, she lost her mother, and her sister got married. She returned to her household and began to look after her father. Her father allowed Eliot to continue her Latin and German lessons.

In 1841, Eliot moved to Coventry, England, with her father. With her school education, her conservative thinking also underwent a change.

In 1850, Eliot decided to become a writer. After her father's death in 1849, she was offered a job as an assistant editor at the *Westminster Review*. Eliot handled most of the work for the company. Her writing was critical and interpretative. Her first three fictional stories were published in *Blackwood's Magazine*.

Eliot was not only a great writer but also an excellent translator. She translated *The Life of Jesus* by David

Strauss from German to English. She published her translation in 1846. In 1854, her translation of Ludwig Andreas Feuerbach's *Essence of Christianity* was also released.

During 1857, she released a short story called *Amos Barton*. She also took on the pen name "George Eliot" to avoid discrimination based on her gender. She compiled three short stories in her next work called *Scenes of Clerical Life*.

She published her first novel, *Adam Bede,* in 1859. It was an instant success. She took inspiration from an anecdote of her aunt's for the main character. Later in the year, she published *The Lifted Veil*, another highly praised success. Her 1860 book *Mill on the Floss* hinted at strong traces of her childhood. The plot was based on the time she spent in small-town, rural England. It played with the theme of religion.

In 1860, Eliot lived in Florence, Italy. She experienced the Renaissance movement. Her next book, *Silas Marner* was issued in 1861. It was used as a school textbook due to its engagement with themes like religion, industrialization and the community. In 1862, her historical fiction novel, *Romola* was released. It wasn't a major commercial success but it is considered to be an important piece of historical fiction.

Eliot's next novel was *Felix Holt,* which was released in 1866. The book was about her own beliefs, and addressed the social issues plaguing England during that period. Her next major work was *Middlemarch,* which came out in 1872. It was published in eight installments. She took the novel from what could potentially have been of mere entertainment value, to a highly intellectual piece of literature.

Eliot came up with her last novel *Daniel Deronda* around 1876. This book was praised by Jewish readers for its sympathetic portrayal of contemporary Jewish characters. It was a fine piece of social satire.

Apart from her literary achievements, she was credited by The Oxford English Dictionary for new words.

After her partner George Lewes' death, Eliot lost all motivation to write. She completed the last volume of Lewes' *Problems of Life and Mind*.She married John Walter Cross on May 6, 1880. The marriage was a short one as Eliot died in London on December 22, 1880, at the age of 61.

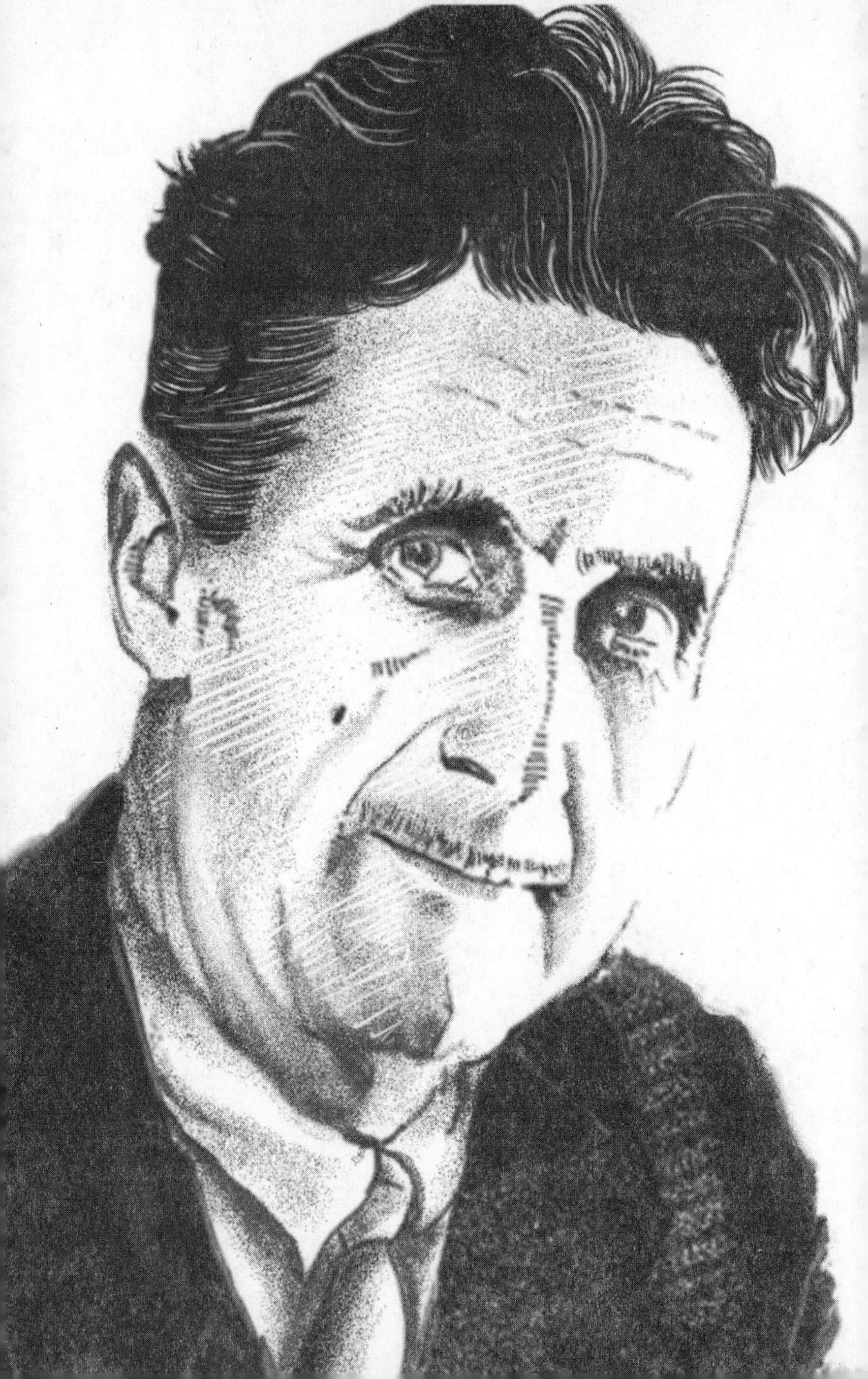

GEORGE ORWELL

BIRTH: *June 25, 1903*
Motihari, India

DEATH: *January 21, 1950 (aged 46)*
London, England

George Orwell was an English novelist, essayist, story-teller, literary critic, advocate and journalist. He fought for political change and was a man of many contradictions. Orwell's best works include the novels *Animal Farm* and *Nineteen Eighty-Four*. These two novels are literary masterpieces and constitute some of the sharpest satirical fiction of the twentieth century.

George Orwell's real name was Eric Arthur Blair.

He was born in 1903 in Bengal, India, to Richard Walmesley Blair and Ida Mabel Blair. His father was an English government official. George was their only son; he had two sisters. He moved to England with his family, when he was one. At the age of five, he composed his first poem. Orwell had a gift for writing, which he recognized very early. When he was eleven, his first poem *Awake Young Men of England* was published in the local newspaper.

In 1911, Orwell attended a preparatory school in Eastbourne, on scholarship. He spent the next five years there. He continued his secondary education at Eton, an elite school, in 1917. At Eton, he took an interest in politics. He was a King's Scholar from 1917 to 1921. He graduated from Eton in 1921.

Orwell joined the Indian Imperial Police in 1922, serving as an officer in Burma. After working for five years, he resigned in 1927 because of his growing dislike for the British rule and returned to England. In the novel *Burmese Days* and the essays *Shooting an Elephant* and *A Hanging,* he describes his life as a police officer and his time in Burma.

In England, he decided to pursue his passion for writing. He struggled financially and also as a writer. He had to do many odd jobs and worked as a teacher at Frays College. In 1929, he moved to London. His experiences with poverty and hardships are mentioned in his first novel, *Down and Out in Paris and London*, which was published in 1933. Before his book was published, he chose the pen name "George Orwell".

In 1934, he published *Burmese Days*. The book talked about British colonialism in Burma. Orwell got more interested in political matters after the success of his novel. The next year, he released *A Clergyman's Daughter*, his most experimental novel. In 1936, Orwell traveled to Spain. He also joined a party called POUM. He was severely injured in the Spanish Civil War. Orwell published *Keep the Aspidistra Flying* in the same year.

From 1937 to 1939, Orwell published many works like *The Road to Wigen Pier, Coming Up for Air* and

Homage to Catalonia. All these novels were based on his observations of Spain and the civil war.

During World War II, he wanted to join the military, but was rejected due to health issues. In 1940, Orwell began writing book reviews for the *New English Weekly*. He also published an essay in three parts called *Inside the Whale*. In 1941, he joined the BBC as a broadcaster and producer for India. Orwell released a lot of books including *The Lion and the Unicorn* during this time. He continued writing reviews for *Time and Tide, Tribune, The Observer, Partisan Review* and *Manchester Evening News*. In 1943, he resigned from the BBC and officially joined *Tribune* as a literary editor, writing more than eighty book reviews.

In 1944, Orwell finished his book *Animal Farm,* the biggest milestone of his literary career. It soon became famous worldwide. After his resignation from the *Tribune,* he became a war correspondent for *The Observer.* He contributed to many smaller political and literary magazines while writing *Nineteen Eighty-Four.* It was published in 1949. Sadly, Orwell did not live to savor the fruits of his success following *Nineteen Eighty-Four.*

Orwell married Eileen Shaughnessy in 1936. The couple had a son. Eileen died in 1945. He remarried Sonia Brownell in 1949, three months before his death. Orwell died from tuberculosis at the age of 46 on January 21, 1950.

Modern readers are often introduced to Orwell as a novelist, mainly through his wildly successful titles *Animal Farm* and *Nineteen Eighty-Four.* In 2008, *The Times* listed him in the list of "50 greatest British writers since 1945".

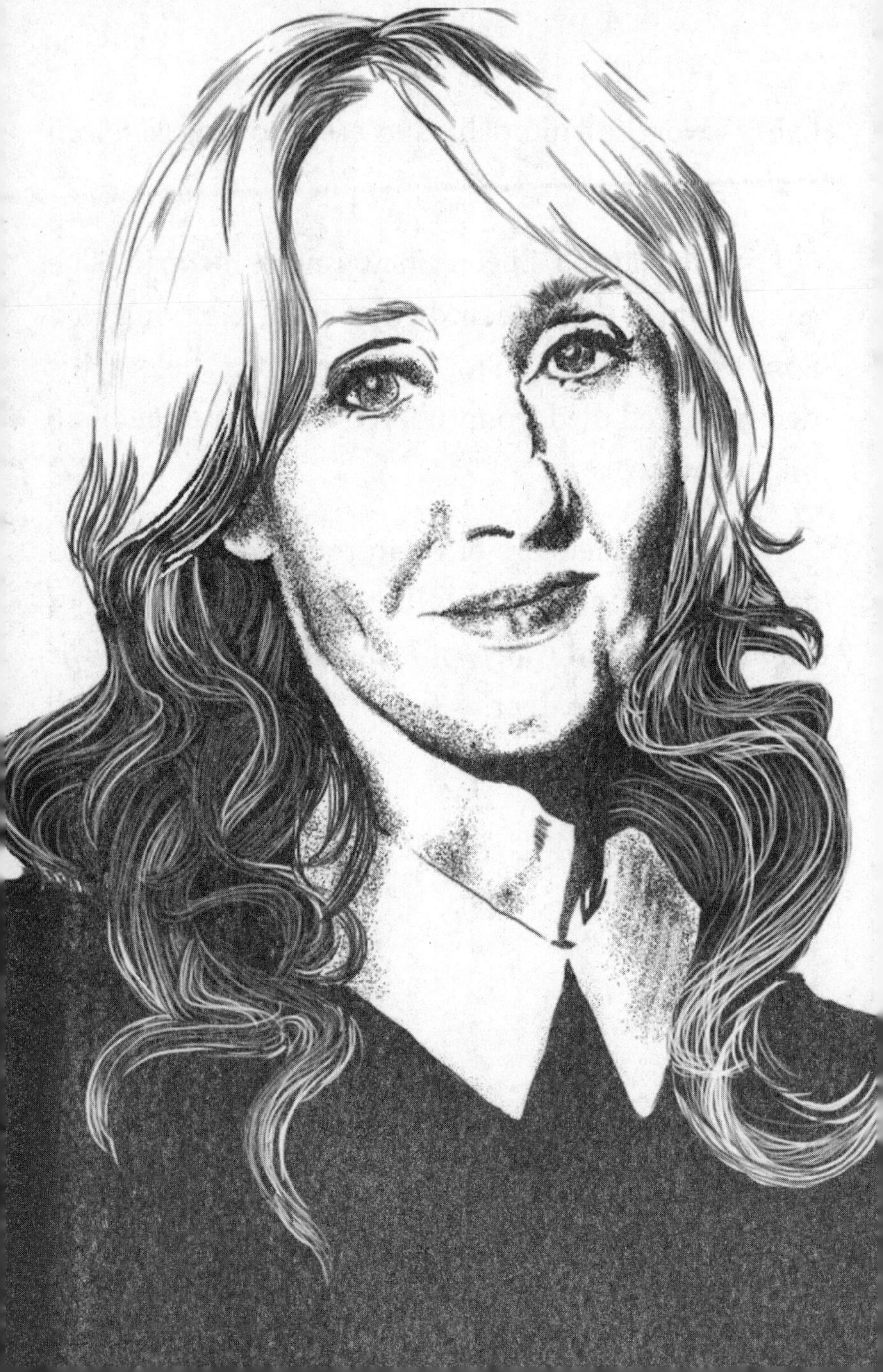

J. K. ROWLING

BIRTH: July 31, 1965
Yate, Gloucestershire, England

J.K. Rowling is amongst the highest-selling authors today. She is the creator of the *Harry Potter* fantasy series, one of the most popular books and film franchises in the world.

Joanne Rowling was born on July 31, 1965, in Yate, England to Peter James Rowling and Anne Rowling. Jo wanted to be a writer from a very early age. She wrote her first book at the age of six. It was a story about a rabbit called *Rabbit*. At the age of eleven, she wrote her first novel about seven cursed diamonds and their owners. She pursued her studies at the University of Exeter and graduated with a BA in French and the classics. After she graduated in 1986, she moved to London. Her first job was that of a researcher, at Amnesty International.

The idea for *Harry Potter* came to her in 1990 on a train ride to London. Soon, she began to plan out all seven books in the series. It took Rowling five years to plan out everything before she started writing *Philosopher's Stone*, the first book of the series. In 1991, she worked as an English teacher. In her free time, she would work on her book. In 1993, Rowling moved to Scotland with her daughter and finished the first three chapters of *Harry Potter and the Philosopher's Stone*. Soon, she had completed her first draft for *Harry Potter and the Philosopher's Stone*. To support her family, she continued to work as a teacher in city schools.

In 1995, in hope of publishing her book, she sent her draft to Christopher Little Literary Agency. Rowling's work was rejected by twelve publishers, before, in 1996, one of the publishers wrote back to her and asked to see the rest of the story. Finally, Bloomsbury published *Harry Potter and the Philosopher's Stone* in 1997. She used the name "J.K. Rowling" for her book. The same year, *Harry Potter and the Philosopher's Stone* was auctioned to Scholastic Inc. in the USA. In 1998, Rowling's book won the Nestle Smarties Book Prize for Children's Book of the Year.

Her second book, titled *Harry Potter and the Chamber of Secrets*, came out in 1998. It became an instant success and was very well received by the readers. Warner Brothers purchased the rights of the first two books to turn the series into movies. The first movie was released in 2001.

In 1999, the third book, *Harry Potter and the Prisoner of Azkaban,* was released. This book also won the Smarties Prize. Rowling is known as the first author to win the prize three times in a row. In 2001, Rowling published two small companion books, *Fantastic Beasts and Where to Find Them* and *Quidditch Through the Ages*.

Queen Elizabeth II of England appointed Rowling an Officer of the Order of the British Empire. The University of Exeter made her an honorary Doctor of Letters in 2000.

Rowling is a humanitarian and donates money to various charities. She supports charities such as Comic Relief and Lumos. In the year 2008, *The Tales of Beedle the Bard* was published in aid of her international children's charity.

In 2002, the next film of the series, *Harry Potter and the Chamber of Secrets* was also released. Another book of the series, *Harry Potter and the Order of the Phoenix* came out the following year, followed by *Harry Potter and the Half-Blood Prince* in 2005.

In 2006, she was named as the most significant living British writer by *The Book Magazine* and the second-richest female entertainer in the world by *Forbes*. In 2007, Rowling finished writing *Harry Potter and the*

Deathly Hallows in a hotel room in Scotland. The book became the fastest-selling book of all time as soon as it released. The Harry Potter series found readers in all age groups.

For her exceptional work, Rowling was awarded the British Books Lifetime Achievement Award, the Edinburgh Award, and the South Bank Show Outstanding Award. In 2012, she launched the digital company 'Pottermore' for her fans. The website includes news, features and articles as well as content by J.K. Rowling herself.

Her works, apart from the Harry Potter series, also gained popularity. In 2012, *The Casual Vacancy* was released. It was translated into more than forty languages and even made into a TV show. Her other works of adult fiction are *The Cuckoo's Calling, Silkworm, Lethal White,* and *Career of Evil.* Rowling's works were also successful because of her fame and popularity. Soon, everyone in the world recognized her for her writing.

In 1992, Rowling married the Portuguese journalist

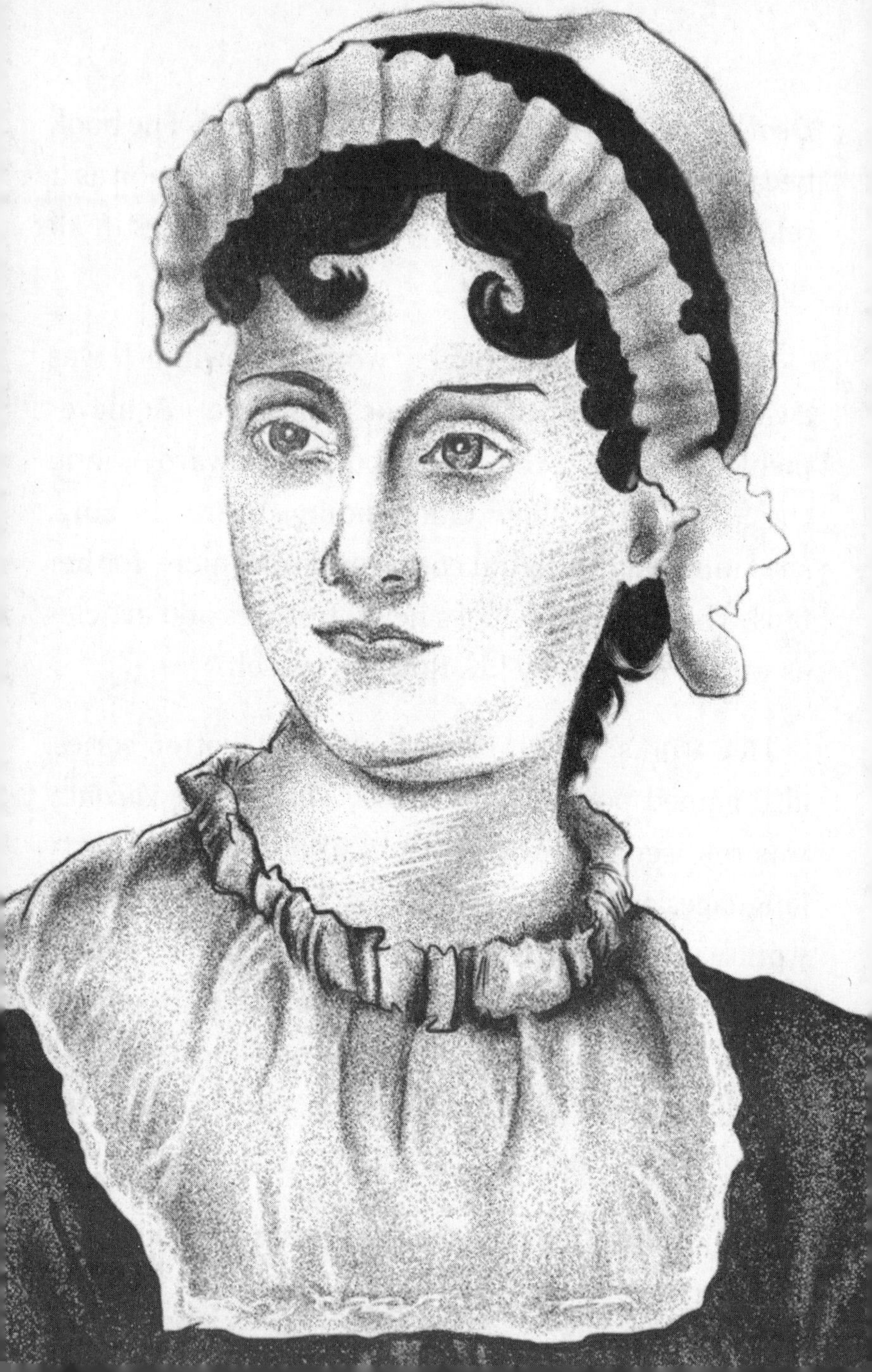

JANE AUSTEN

BIRTH: *December 16, 1775*
Steventon, England

DEATH: *July 18, 1817 (aged 41)*
Winchester, England

Jane Austen is one of the most famous novelists in English literature. Her books are considered as classics and her most admired work was her novel *Pride and Prejudice*.

Jane Austen was born on December 16, 1775, in Steventon, England, to George Austen and Cassandra Leigh Austen. The family was tightly knit. Both her parents were from different social backgrounds. Her mother belonged to a higher social rank than her father. Jane's mother did not seem to regret her decision to marry her husband though. However, this divide is a common theme in Austen's novels. Most characters in her stories belonged to different social classes.

Jane was particularly close to her sister Cassandra and her brother Henry. Her brother Henry had a great circle of friends. He exposed her to a society that she would not have known otherwise. A few years later, he became Jane's literary agent.

She taught herself how to speak Italian and French and learned the piano. In her teen years, Austen wrote poems and stories to entertain her family. She honed her comic skills by writing for her family members. She drafted her many articles into three bound notebooks. She published all three in a compilation titled *Juvenalia*. It consists of 29 plays, verses and short novels.

Austen expressed an interest in theatre and comedy as a kid. She used to do theatrical productions at home with her siblings. Austen's early works include a comic novel with the intentionally misspelt title *Love and Freindship*, *Lady Susan* and the satire *The History of England*.

Austen published her first novel, *Sense and Sensibility* in 1811. Though she had already started working on her novel, *First Impressions* after a short romance. This book turned into the ever-popular *Pride and Prejudice* but it was published after *Sense and Sensibility*, in 1813. The book took her years to write. The story explained how first impressions and pride could lead to prejudice. Her next published book was Northanger Abbey. It was actually the first book she completed, back in 1803, however, it wasn't published until after her death in 1817. The story was full of mysteries which took place in Northanger Abbey. This novel achieved great success.

Mansfield Park was published in 1814. It was the story of a poor girl Fanny Price, raised by her wealthy aunt and uncle at Mansfield Park. Many critics praised her novel and called it the "first modern novel". In 1816, she released *Emma*. Critics liked the eponymous character and praised it—as her most complex one so far.

Her final novel, *Persuasion* was published in 1818. It was a romantic novel revolving around the characters Anne Elliott and Captain Wentworth.

At the age of twenty, she met Tom Lefroy, a young Irishman. They seemed to like each other. However, Lefroy's family sent him back home to break the engagement, since Austen was from a poor household, thus ending the brief romance. Her interest in love and marriage led her to meet the wealthy Harris Bigg-Wither at the age of 27. He proposed to her and Austen accepted. But this time, she broke the engagement, as she was worried that she had accepted him for comfort, rather than love. Thus, she remained unmarried for life. But all her novels were concentrated heavily on the themes of marriage and courtship. In fact, some of her works also deal with the dilemma of marrying for love or comfort.

Austen's personal life revolved around her family

and close friends. She thrived as a warm and loving aunt. In early 1816, she started suffering from Addison's Disease. However, she continued to write and revised her work, *The Elliots* and started work on *Sandition*, which remained incomplete. She died on July 8, 1817, at the age of 41.

Towards the end of the nineteenth century, Austen gained a significant amount of admirers known as "Janeites". After her death, modern authors wrote a sequel to *Pride and Prejudice* and endings for *Sandition*. Till date, hundreds of literary and cinematic adaptations of Austen's novels have been made.

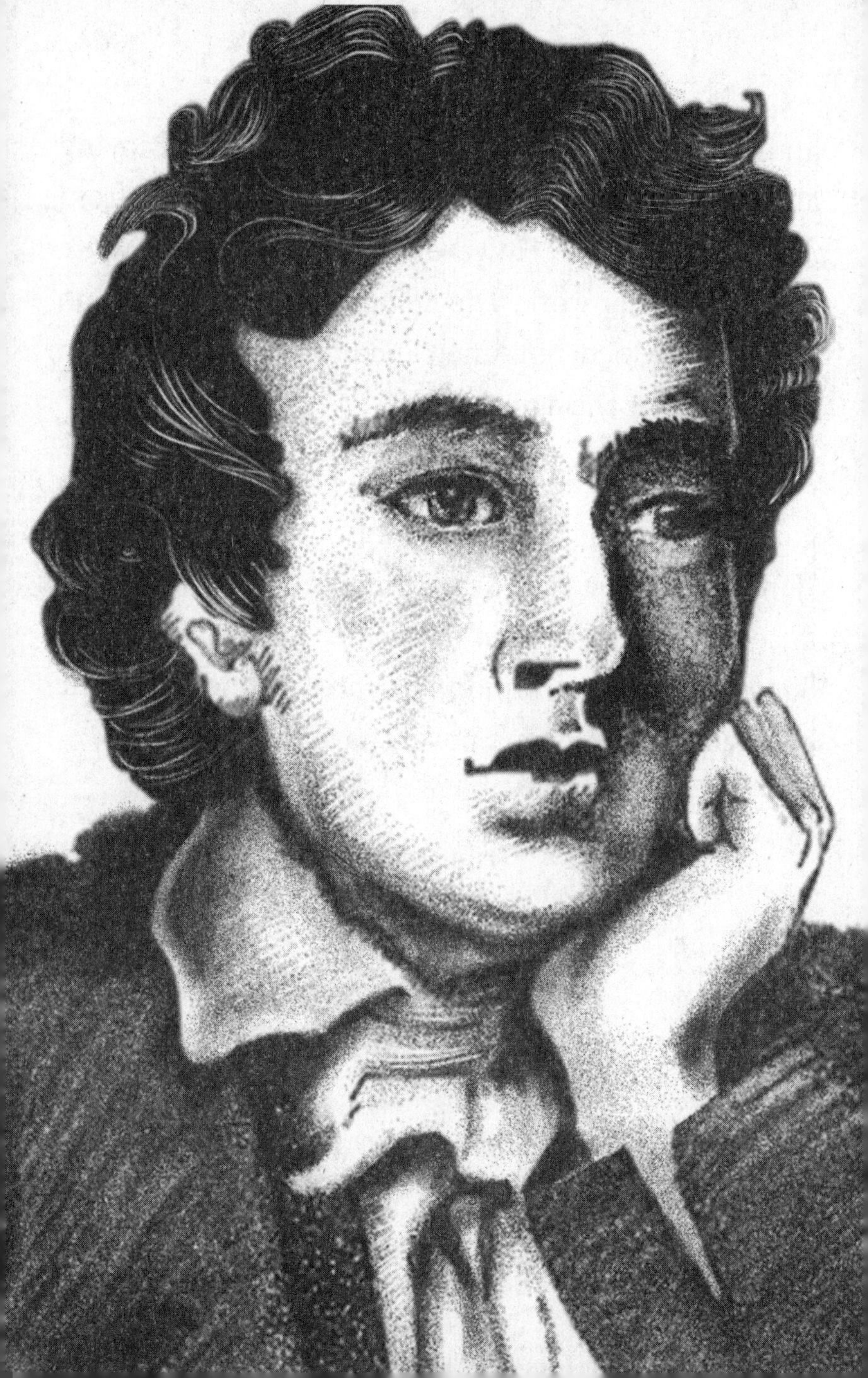

JOHN KEATS

BIRTH: October 31, 1795
London, England

DEATH: February 23, 1821 (aged 25)
Rome, Italy

John Keats was an English lyric poet. He was one of the most important figures of the second generation of Romantic poets.

John Keats was born on October 31, 1795, in London, to Thomas and France Keats. He had three siblings. In 1803, he attended John Clarke's School. He took an interest in classic literature and history. At a very young age, he lost both his parents. His father died in 1804 when John was eight; his mother died of tuberculosis when John was fourteen. During his time at John Clarke's school, he found solace and comfort in art and literature. He became close to his headmaster John Clarke's son. His headmaster encouraged his interest in poetry and literature. Keats' grandmother took custody of the children. At the age of sixteen, he was an apprentice for the surgeon, Dr Hammond in Edmonton.

Even though he loved writing and reading poems, he continued to work hard towards becoming a surgeon. In 1814, Keats wrote *Imitation of Spenser*. It was his first step towards a writing career. In 1815, Keats entered Guy's Hospital for his medical training. But he soon gave up his medical career and decided to become a poet.

Keats met Joseph Severn, a young painter who later accompanied him to Rome. Keats also met William Haslam, who became one of his closest friends. Keats published his first poem, *To Solitude* in 1815. It was also published in *The Examiner* and was well-received by people. He met Leigh Hunt, publisher of *The Examiner* who later became a vital part of Keats' literary career. Hunt introduced him to English poets such as Percy Bysshe Shelley and William Wordsworth. In 1816, John wrote *On First Looking into Chapman's Homer*, which earned him the much-deserved reputation of being a good poet. He wrote his next book on the subject of poverty. Even though the book was not well-received, it didn't stop him from writing. Keats' *Sleep and Poetry* and was written around the same time. The poem ended with the notion of a 'brotherhood'.

The same year, he started to show signs of tuberculosis. In 1817, Keats' first volume of poetry *Poems* was published by the Ollier Brothers. The book didn't sell very well. In 1818, Keats began to work on his long poem, *Endymion*. He called his poems "a trial of my powers of imagination". It was a four-thousand-line poem based on the Greek myth of the same name. He finished his other work, *Isabella, or the Pot of Basil*, in 1820. Keats spent 1818 taking care of his brother Tom, who was in the final stages of tuberculosis. It was the same disease that had killed their mother. Later, he met the eighteen-year-old Fanny Brawne in Hampstead, and fell in love with her.

In 1819, Keats moved to London with his friend, Charles Brown. He published *Isabella*, a poem about a woman who fell in love with a man who was below her social rank. The same year, he finished *The Eve of St Agnes* and dropped his first version of *Hyperion*, based on a Greek myth. He took no breaks and kept on writing, producing works like the *Ode to Psyche, Ode to a Nightingale* and *Ode to Melancholy*. While he was in England, he released one of his most beautiful works, *To Autumn*. It was based on the ripening of fruit, the sleepy workers and the maturing sun accompanying the season of Autumn. The poem showed Keats' true writing style. In 1820, his final volume of *Lamia, Isabella, The Eve of St Agnes, and Other Poems* was published. After that, his health started to deteriorate, yet he continued working.

Most of his works were inspired by his own

relationships. It was claimed that Keats wrote Fanny Brawne a love sonnet, *Bright Star*, in which he declared his love for her.

John Keats died of tuberculosis at the age of 25, in Rome, on 23rd February, 1821. He was buried in the Protestant cemetery in Rome. On his tombstone, the words "Here lies one whose name was writ in water" were carved at his request. He was a Romantic at heart, and the same was seen in his poetry.

Keats' houses in Wentworth Palace and Rome were turned into memorials, as a tribute to the great poet. His letters and manuscripts were archived at the Harvard University library, British Library and in Keats House. The British Keats-Shelley Memorial Association was founded for the School of Romantic Poetry.

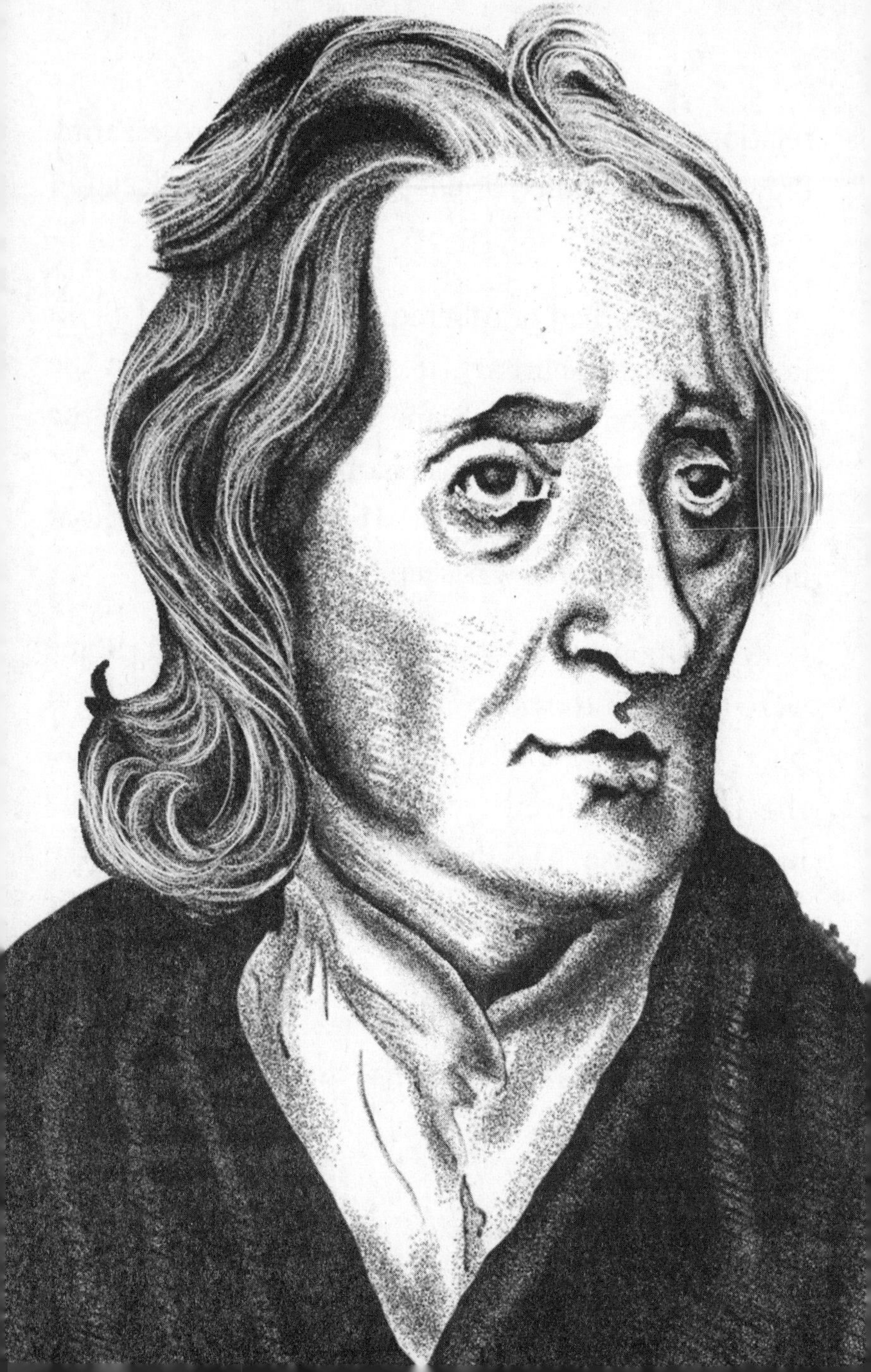

JOHN LYLY

BIRTH: 1554, Kent, England

DEATH: November 1606
London, England

John Lyly was an English writer, poet and dramatist. He was best-known for his prose romances.

John Lyly was born in 1554 in Kent, England, to Peter Lyly and Jane Burgh. He was the first of eight children. At the age of sixteen, Lyly attended Magdalen College in Oxford. He got his bachelor's and master's degrees in 1573 and 1575. Throughout his master's studies, Lyly gained fame for his first two prose publications. They were *Euphues: The Anatomy of Wit* and *Euphues and His England*.

These famous fictional books describe the adventures of a Greek scholar named Euphues. It was written in the epistolary style. His exact arrangement and selection of words, frequent use of similes drawn from classical mythology, and his artificial and elegant prose came to be known as "Euphuism", which though short-lived, quickly caught on amongst writers.

In the 1580s, Lyly began to write comedies and plays. In 1583, he gained control of the Blackfriars Theatre. He used the theater to produce his earliest plays like *Campaspe,* and *Sapho and Phao.* Except for *The Woman in the Moon,* all his comedies were done by the company the Children of Paul. The company was favored by Queen Elizabeth. That time, eight of Lyly's plays were performed before the Queen. All the plays were only performed by male actors.

Lyly's *Endymion* was seen as a masterpiece. Lyly's

plays were known as the stepping stone to improving English dramas. His plots were based on the classical mythology and legends of the time. There was beauty and wit in his dialogues.

Lyly polished his writing skills with the help of Oxford. His work began to be credited as soon as he started work with Oxford. His writing was a combination of old humor with the modern genre. Lyly was always interested in classical characters. He often used Greek legends as an inspiration for his books. He usually mixed prose and verse in his writing. The phrase "All is fair in love and war" was associated with Lyly's *Euphues*. It is now a staple in our vocabularies.

Lyly's most successful years were from 1584 to 1601. He wrote most of his plays and comedies during this period. Even William Shakespeare's plays, mainly the romantic comedies, were influenced by Lyly's work. His *Love's Metamorphosis* was an important source for Shakespeare's *A Midsummer Night's Dream*. In 2007, Primavera Productions in London staged the reading of Lyly's *Gallathea*, which was later linked to Shakespeare's plays.

Lyly also produced an "entertainment" (a show that combined elements of masque and drama) for Queen Elizabeth. The most famous one was *The Entertainment at Mitcham*, performed in 1598. Lyly wrote the dialogue for the entire show. He became a member of the parliament in 1580, and represented three different constituencies over the years.

Lyly continued to write throughout his life. His popularity faded with the rise of the great writers of the time like Thomas Kyd, Christopher Marlowe and William Shakespeare. He had to request financial support from Queen Elizabeth. However, he didn't get the support he needed and went unnoticed. His influence as a writer also decreased. Lyly died in November 1606, in London, England. He died poor and neglected in the early part of James I's reign. There were some petty records of his family life and some letters, which explained how he was overlooked later in life.

He was a pioneering English writer and playwright during the Elizabethan period. His innovative ways in English prose and theater were an inspiration for a generation of younger playwrights like Christopher Marlowe and William Shakespeare. He left a lasting impression on the English language and literature.

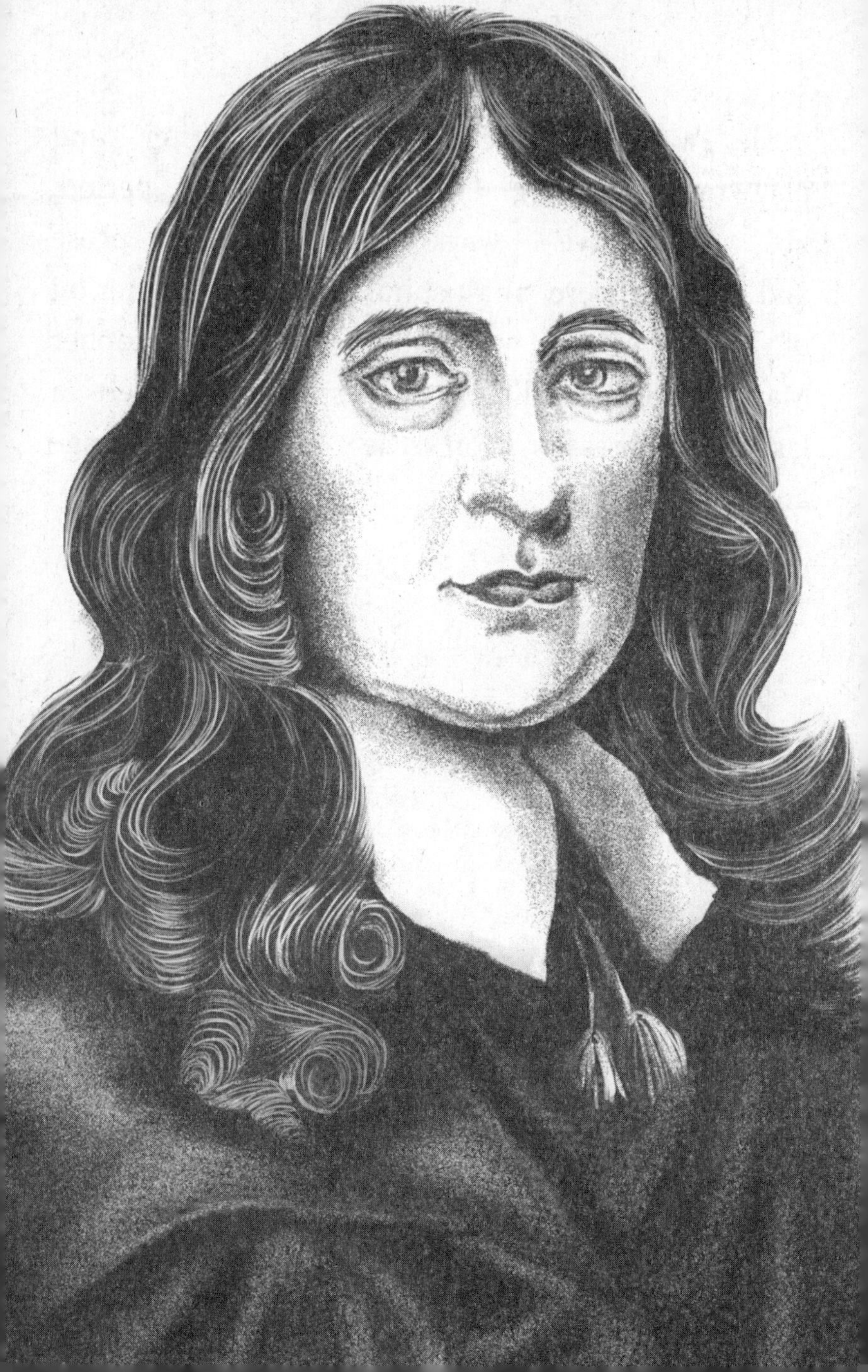

JOHN MILTON

BIRTH: *December 9, 1608*
London, England

DEATH: *November 8, 1674*
Chalfont St. Giles, England

John Milton was an English poet, essayist and historian. He was considered the most notable English author after William Shakespeare.

John Milton was born in London on Dec- ember 9, 1608 to John and Sara Milton. Milton composed beautiful pieces and some hymns that are still sung in this century. He was tutored privately and later attended St Paul's School. He studied different languages like Latin, Greek, Italian, Hebrew, French and Spanish. At the age of fifteen, he went to Christ College, Cambridge. He graduated with a Bachelor of Arts degree in 1629, and a Master of Arts degree in 1632.

After he graduated, he returned to his home in London. Three years later, Milton's family relocated to Buckinghamshire because of the plague outbreak. He kept himself busy with studies and participated in social and cultural events held in his hometown. Milton began to read mainly Latin and Greek authors. His first major written piece was *On the Death of a Fair Infant, Dying of the Cough*. It was about the death of his sister's child in 1628. Soon he'd written *On the Morning of Christ's Nativity, On Shakespeare, Il Penserosi* and *L'Allegro*.

For 15 months around 1638, Milton traveled around Italy and France. While he was in Florence, Milton met Galileo. Till date, the reason why Milton met the blind astronomer is unknown. He is the only contemporary mentioned by name in *Paradise Lost*. Milton mentioned his meeting with Galileo in his

1644 pamphlet *Areopagitica*.

Even as a puritan and a believer of the Bible, he questioned religious institutions like the Church. He wrote about themes like freedom of the press. He was also one of the supporters of the English Civil War. He even wrote a formal publication for Cromwell's government. Gradually, he started to lose his eyesight. By the time he wrote *Paradise Lost*, he'd completely lost his eyesight. It became difficult for him to finish the work, but it wasn't enough to make him stop writing.

John Milton published some plots which reflected his concerns about the state-ruled Church. *A Treatise of Civil Power* was published in 1659, in which he requested the separation of Church and State. In *Ready and Easy Way*, he supported a government structure where the citizens would be free to vote.

He started his first edition of *Paradise Lost* in 1667. He published it in a ten-book edition. *Paradise Lost* is an epic, free-form English poem. The plot drew from Biblical themes. It is remembered as Milton's greatest epic. The epic narrates how Satan influenced Adam and Eve. Later in the story, Adam and Eve are banished from the Garden of Eden. Even though Milton wanted to highlight brotherly love among all, the tone of his magnum opus seemed to favor Satan, rather than God, for some critics. His works were criticized by people and poets all around the world.

In 1671, Milton's last two poems were published in one volume. *Paradise Regained*, a brief epic in four books, was followed by *Samson Agonistes,* a dramatic poem that was not meant for the stage.

Milton also had an interest in politics. He fought for human rights and was against the rule of English leaders. As a writer, he expressed his activism by writing long and careful debates to put forth his point of view. Milton believed that the social hierarchy that existed in his day was corrupted. In his lifetime, he wrote treatises on subjects regarding the Church, monarchy, free press, freedom of religion and expression, and divorce.

Milton married three times and was the father of three children. He died on November 8, 1674, in England.

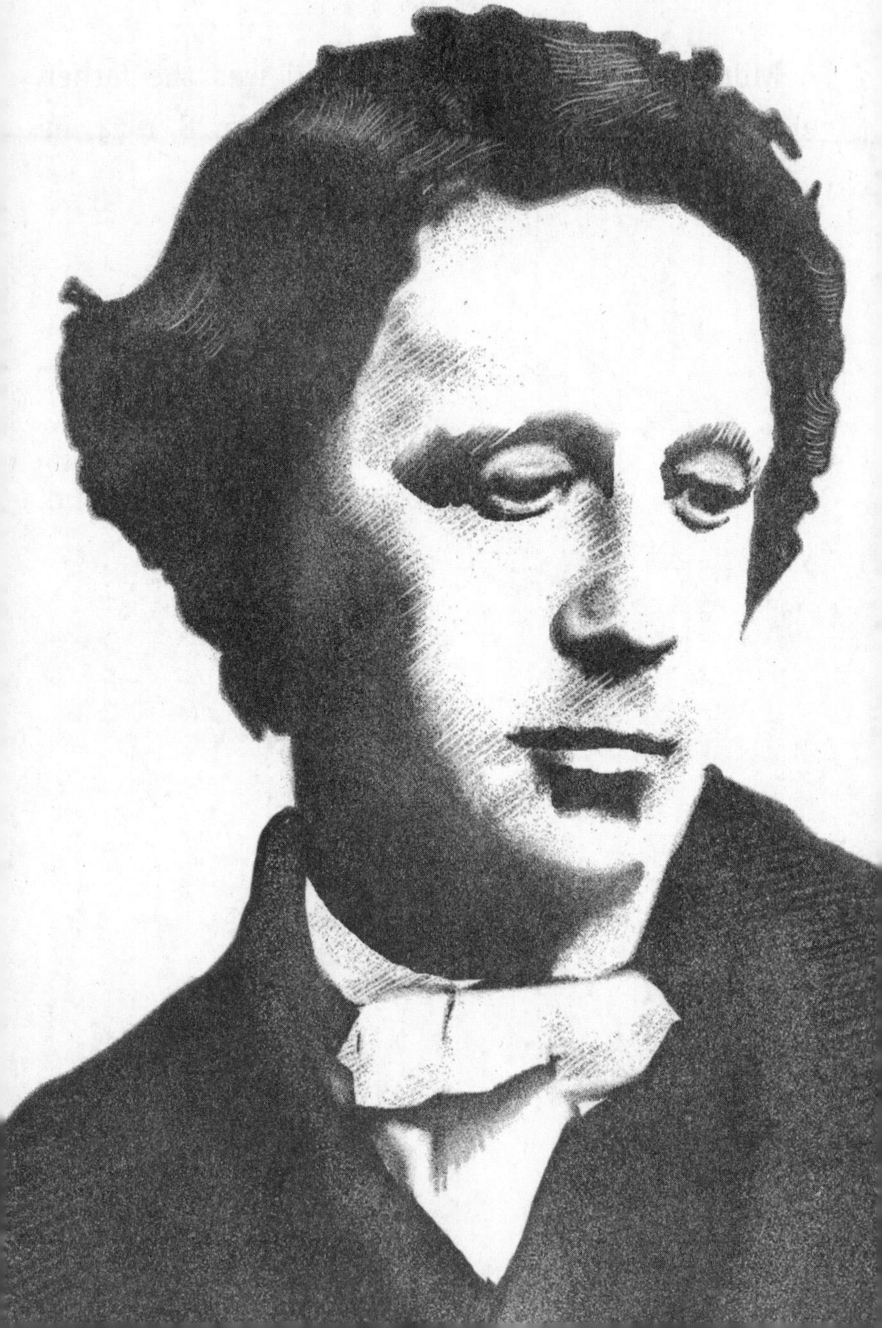

LEWIS CARROLL

BIRTH: *January 27, 1832*
Daresbury, England

DEATH: *January 14, 1898 (aged 65)*
Guildford, England

Lewis Carroll was a famous English writer, mathematician and photographer. Carroll's most famous works were *Alice in Wonderland* and *Through the Looking Glass,* two of the most revered literary texts till date. He wrote many adventure stories for children that adults also thoroughly enjoyed.

Lewis Carroll's real name was Charles Lutwidge Dodgson. He was born on 27th January, 1832 in Daresbury, England to Frances Jane Lutwidge and

Reverend Charles Dodgson. He was the third of eleven children. His father was a priest in the Church of England and they lived in Yorkshire, England for 25 years. From a very young age, he had an interest in mathematics and writing.

In 1844, he attended the Richmond Grammar School at the age of twelve. Later, he went to Rugby School in 1846. Carroll suffered from a fever, which resulted in a deaf ear. He also stammered, and was bullied while in Rugby School. In 1851, he went to Christ Church at Oxford University to pursue studies in classics and mathematics. After he graduated, he became a mathematics lecturer at Christ Church. He resigned from his teaching job in 1881.

Carroll's writing career began at a very young age. He started by writing short stories and poetry. He compiled some of his writing in *The Rectory Umbrella* around 1850. He also put together a magazine called the *Useful and Instructive Poetry*, for his family. His writing was funny and sarcastic.

His major work was based on the people he admired a lot in his life. He was a friend of the new Dean of Christ Church, Henry Liddell. Through him, he got to know the Dean's children, Lorina, Edith and Alice. His muse was the last child, who he used as the main character in *Alice's Adventures in Wonderland*, released by Macmillan Publishers in 1865. He gained immense fame for this. The book became a global bestseller. In 1871, he published its sequel called *Through the Looking-Glass and What Alice Found There*. The Alice series recounts the adventures of a little girl who falls, through a rabbit hole, into a fantasy world. It is some of the most loved and celebrated children's fiction in the world.

Carroll remained a teacher even after his success as a writer. In 1876, he published a poem called *The Hunting of the Snark*. It was also a huge success. He released another book in 1895 titled *Sylvie and Bruno*. But it wasn't as successful as his previous fiction works.

As an introvert, he was unable to maintain his friendships with adults. He spent most of his time playing with and entertaining children. The central theme of all his books were children, and he created stories for them.

He started to take an interest in photography during 1856. In 1860, he visited his birthplace and took photos of people and places he knew as a kid. He soon became famous as a photographer and as an artist, too. He made portraits of famous people such as Ellen Terry, Dante Lord Salisbury, Lord Alfred Tennyson and many more. In 1880, he gave up photography when he realized that he was no longer passionate about it.

Carroll was also recognized as an inventor. He invented 'The Wonderland Postage-Stamp Case' in 1889. He also improved letter writing, for which he designed a writing tablet called the 'Nyctograph'. This machine helped people take notes in the dark. He also created many brain-teaser word games. He developed rules to explain the right margins on a typewriter; he also established the rules of tennis tournaments. He even created a double-sided sticky strip to seal envelopes.

Carroll remained unmarried because he wanted to become a priest earlier in life. He died at the age of 66 on 14th January, 1898, after suffering from pneumonia and influenza. He was buried at the Mount Cemetery in Guildford.

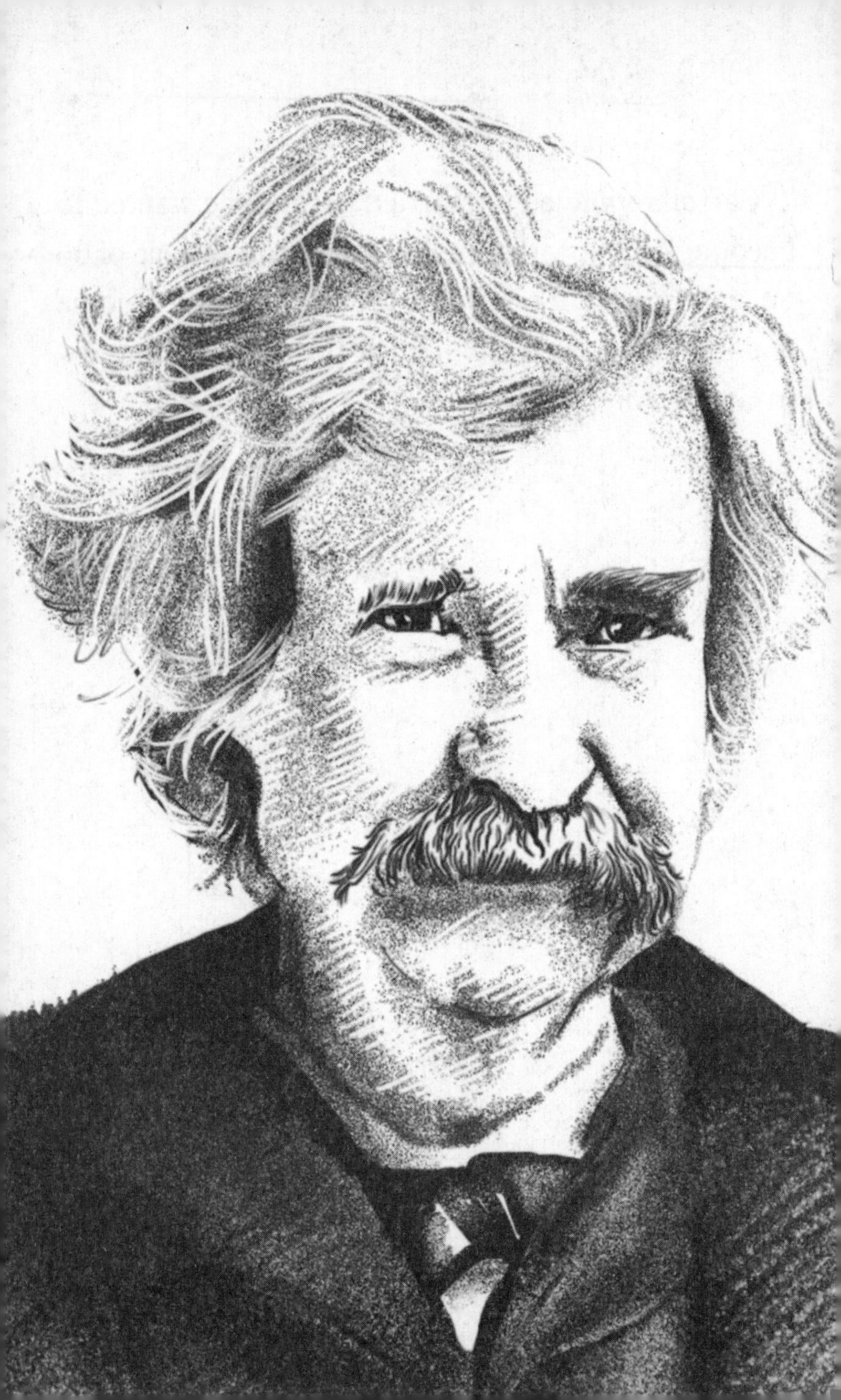

MARK TWAIN

BIRTH: November 30, 1835
Florida, Missouri, USA

DEATH: April 21, 1910 (aged 74)
Connecticut, USA

Mark Twain was an American author, essayist and humorist. He was known as the 'Father of American Literature'.

Mark Twain's real name was Samuel Langhorne Clemens. He was born in Florida, Missouri on November 30, 1835 to Jane and John Marshall Clemens. When Twain was about four, his family moved to Hannibal, Missouri, a small town of about five hundred people, in search of better business opportunities. He was born two months premature and hence was a weak child. As a baby, he wasn't expected to live a long life. His father died of pneumonia in 1847. When Twain lost his father, his family fell into a financial crisis. Twain had to work very hard to support his family.

At the age of eleven, Twain dropped out of school and became a printer's assistant. He started to work as a typesetter in 1851. He occasionally contributed articles and humorous sketches in the *Hannibal Journal*, a local newspaper owned by his brother, Orion. He eventually wrote a handful of short, satirical items for the publication. In 1853, a seventeen-year-old Twain left Hannibal. He traveled to places like New York City, Philadelphia and Keokuk, Iowa, and also continued to work as a printer.

When Twain was 21, he achieved his dream of becoming a steamboat man. He was thrilled when the steamboat pilot, Horace E. Bixby took him on as a student. Every day, he was trained in navigation on the Mississippi River. He was employed on a boat called 'Pennsylvania'. After more than two years of harsh training, Twain became a licensed river pilot in 1859. He was satisfied with his job and earned good money. However, his stint was cut short when the American civil war broke out. Most of the civilian traffic on the river and the river trade was affected. Twain was forced to find an alternative job.

Twain left Missouri and traveled west with his brother Orion. He struggled to re-establish himself and his career. He tried his luck at silver mining. This job did not suit him. So, he decided to become a reporter for a Virginia City news- paper in 1862. During this time, Twain chose the pen name "Mark Twain", a riverman's slang for water that is just safe enough for navigation. He published some of his letters and accounts of travel in five travelogues. He narrated his experiences about his visit to the Western US and Asia. These were later put into collections like the *Letters from Honolulu* and others.

He first enjoyed success as a writer in 1865.

His witty story, *Jim Smiley and His Jumping Frog*, was published in the New York weekly, *The Saturday Press*. In 1870, he became the editor and part-owner of the *Buffalo Express* in New York.

In 1876, he released his masterpiece *The Adventures of Tom Sawyer*. It was about a young boy, Tom Sawyer, growing up alongside the Mississippi River. The book, a heart-warming tale of a young boy's adventures, became a huge success. In 1881, Twain published the novel *The Prince and the Pauper*. It was his first attempt at historical fiction. The story was about two young boys who are identical in appearance. The novel inspired numerous theatrical productions and films.

Twain's novel, *The Adventures of Huckleberry Finn* was published in 1884 and cemented his reputation as an author of international repute.

Twain established himself as a successful writer, but failed as a businessman. Twain lost loads of money in some poor investments and ultimately went bankrupt.

Alexander Graham Bell also offered him the chance to invest in his telephone invention. Sadly, Twain turned down the offer. He filed for bankruptcy in 1894. His friend came to his aid at this difficult time and helped him re-establish himself financially.

Twain was also a featured speaker. He did many solo humorous performances and gave speeches in men's clubs.

When he served as a steamboat man, Twain met Charles Langdon, who introduced him to his sister, Olivia. Twain and Olivia married in 1870. They had four children and were happily married.

Twain died of a heart attack on April 21, 1910 at the age of 74, during the appearance of Haley's Comet, which had coincidentally also occurred during the time of his birth.

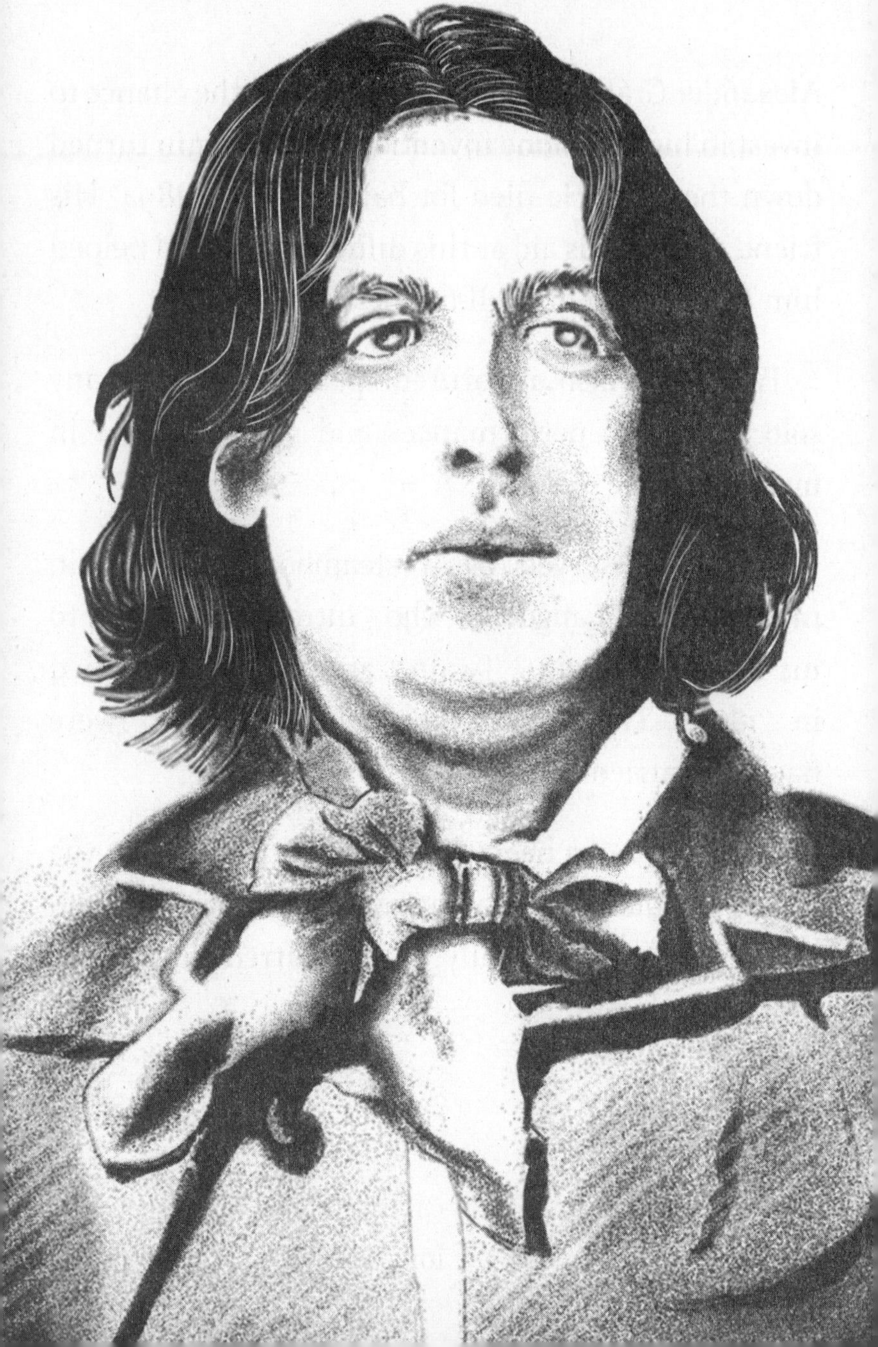

OSCAR WILDE

BIRTH: October 16, 1854,
Dublin, Ireland

DEATH: November 30, 1900 (aged 46),
Paris, France

Oscar Wilde was an Anglo-Irish playwright, novelist, poet and critic. He is considered as one of the greatest playwrights of the Victorian Era.

Oscar Fingal O'Flahertie Wills Wilde was born on October 16, 1854 in Dublin, Ireland to Sir William Wilde and Jane Wilde. His father was a well-known doctor.

At the age of eleven, he went to Portora Royal School. Wilde started taking an interest in all things

Greek. He also won several prizes as he was good at academics. After he graduated he went to Trinity College, Dublin. There, he not only excelled in studies but also composed Greek verses. He received the Berkeley Gold Medal for Greek and the Demyship scholarship for further studies at Magdalen College in Oxford. In 1874, he went to Oxford. There, he won the Newdigate Prize for his poem *Ravenna*. His four years at Oxford were fruitful for his writing career. He was involved in the Aesthetic movement and became an advocate for the 'Art for Art's Sake' perspective.

In 1879, he moved to London to start his literary career. He published his first collection called *Poems* in 1880. His first play, *Vera* was performed in 1883. He received mixed reviews for this. The next year, he traveled to New York. He gave lectures in the United States and Canada and delivered hundreds of lectures in just nine months. His tour was successful and he earned enough money to spend three months in Paris. He finished writing his play *The Duchess of Padua* while there.

Wilde accepted the position of an editor at *Lady's World* magazine in 1885. He expanded the magazine to include women's viewpoints on art, music, literature and modern life, instead of merely focusing on what they wear. He openly supported women's rights and wanted the society to take them seriously.

In 1888, he wrote *The Happy Prince and Other Tales*. It was a collection of tales written for his children. In 1889, he penned an essay called *The Decay of Lying*, which contained characters named after his sons, Vivian and Cyril. In 1891, he wrote his first and only novel, *The Picture of Dorian Gray*. While the novel is now considered to be a masterpiece, it was condemned for its lack of morality when it was first released. Wilde, in one of the most sensational prefaces ever, defended his work using the argument of aestheticism.

Wilde's first successful play was called *Lady Windermere's Fan*, released in 1892. He worked on some of the most successful comedies soon after, like *A Woman of No Importance*, *The Importance of Being Earnest* and *An Ideal Husband*, which revolved around the themes of blackmail and political corruption. These plays were all highly praised by audiences and critics alike. The success of his plays strongly established Wilde as a playwright.

Wilde was at the height of his theatrical success in 1895. But, the same year, he was arrested for homosexuality, which was against the law at the time. Wilde was sentenced to two years of hard labor. He faced a very hard time while he was in jail. Wilde got rejected by his friends, his book sales went down, his plays were shut down, and his belongings were sold off at an auction at low prices. But he never stopped writing. He wrote *De Profundis* (fully published in 1905), a dramatic monologue, as a letter to a friend and a formal defense. In 1897, he published *The Ballad of Reading Gaol*.

Oscar Wilde married Constance Lloyd, daughter of a wealthy adviser of the Queen in 1884. The couple had two sons.

He spent most of his life in Europe. He lived in cheap

hotels and enjoyed real success as a writer only in the last decade of his relatively short life. Wilde was best recognized for his last play *The Importance of Being Earnest*, a comedy that plays with double identities.

He died on November 30, 1900, at the age of 46 in a hotel in Paris. Sadly, it was only after his death that he became widely known for his literary accomplishments and his witty and imaginative works.

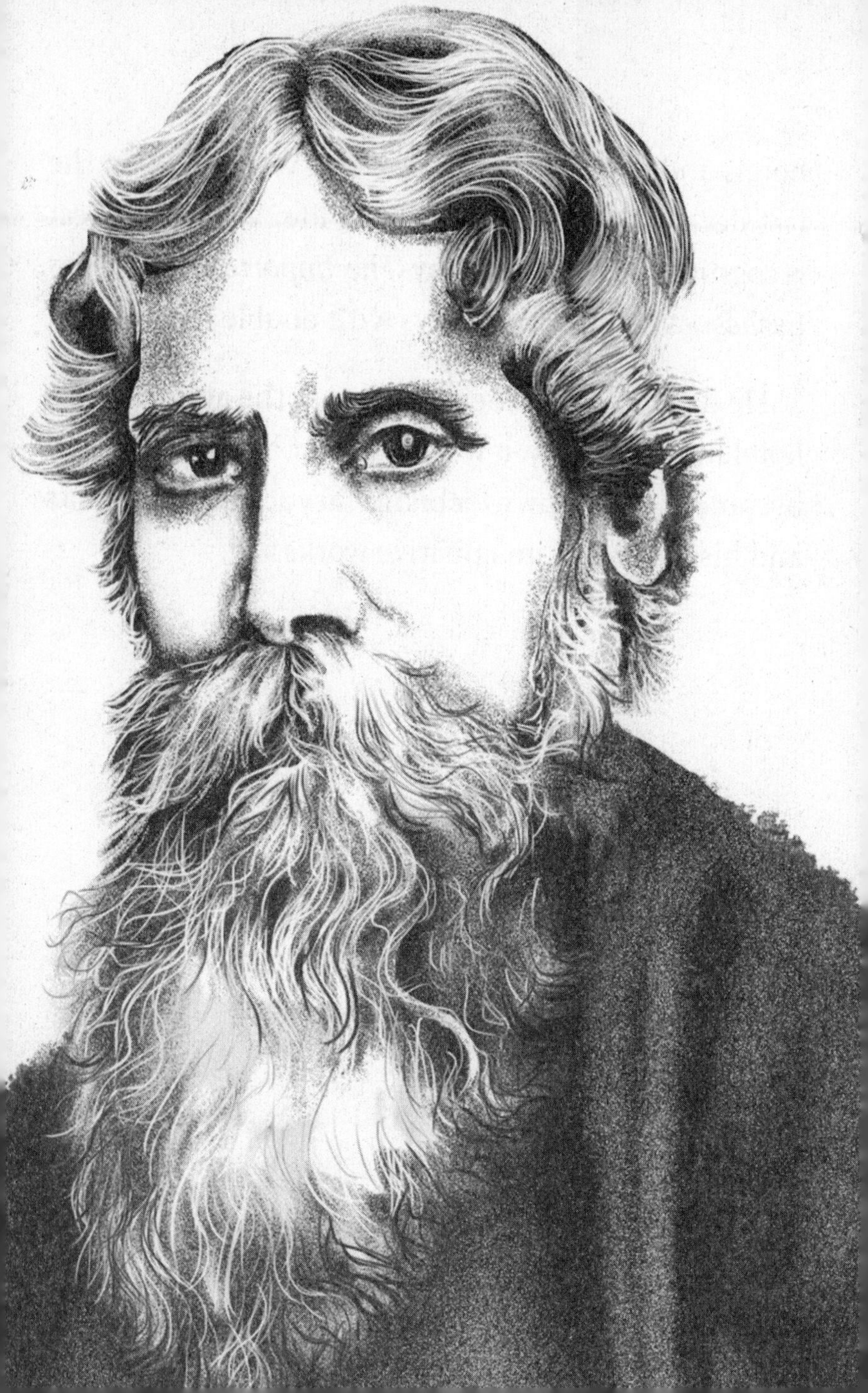

RABINDRANATH TAGORE

BIRTH: May 7, 1861
Kolkata, India

DEATH: August 7, 1941 (aged 80)
Kolkata, India

Rabindranath Tagore was one of the most significant literary figures of the twentieth century. He was a widely acclaimed wordsmith in India. He was known as 'Gurudev' or the poet of poets.

Rabindranath Thakur (Tagore) was born on May 7, 1861, in Kolkata, India, to Debendranath Tagore and Sarada Devi. He was the fourteenth of fifteen children and was fondly referred to as "Rabi". He lost his mother at a very young age. His father was a philosopher and leader of the Bengali religious group 'Brahmo Samaj'. While Rabi himself wanted to attend school, he was mostly home-schooled by his father. At the age of seventeen, he was sent to England where he got his formal schooling.

Tagore moved to Brighton, England for his higher studies. He was exposed to the world of theater, music and literature. He started to read Shakespeare's works. But Tagore returned to Bengal without a formal degree.

When Tagore was eleven, he frequently traveled around India with his father. During this time, he took an interest in poetry. He read a lot of Kalidasa's works, who was a classical Sanskrit poet. Tagore also studied works of other famous writers. Their writing inspired Tagore to pursue his own writing career. In 1877, he composed a long poem in the Maithili style.

His goal was to blend the Bengali and European traditions in his literary pieces. In 1882, he wrote one of his most famous poems, *Nirjharer Swapnabhanga*.

In 1890, a collection of his poems, *Manasi* was published. The poems displayed his exceptional writing skills. He combined social and political satire that was critical of his fellow Bengalis. Tagore had an early breakthrough as a writer in his native place, Bengal.

1891-95 were Tagore's most fruitful years as a writer. He released the three-volume long *Galpaguchchha*. It was a collection of eighty short stories, which covered topics like poverty, the caste-system, illiteracy, marriage and the lives of rural Bengalis.

In 1901, he moved to rural Bengal, where most of his major works were written, and founded an ashram named Shantiniketan, meaning "abode of peace". A few years later, he published *Kheya*. He wrote many great novels including *Gora*. *Gora* is considered as one of the greatest works in Bengali literature. He traveled to England for a third time and took his translated works with him. Tagore began to present his works and soon it caught the interest of some notable writers of the time like William Butler Yeats, Ezra Pound, Robert Bridges, Ernest Rhys and Thomas Sturge Moore.

Tagore's significant works included *Gitanjali: Song Offerings*, which was translated into English and published in England, receiving a very positive response. With the success of his book, Tagore's popularity grew internationally. The central themes of his works revolved around life and society, which were very universal themes.

Tagore was also the founder of 'Visva-Bharati' at Shantiniketan. The main aim of this organization was to unite the East and West culturally.

Tagore was a great patriot and had immense love for his country. He received knighthood in 1915, which he gave up in 1919 after the Jallianwallah Bagh massacre. Even Gandhiji called Tagore his Gurudev and considered him to be the master of love, peace and culture. Tagore had mutual admiration for Gandhi and gave him the title 'Mahatma'.

Tagore composed around 2000 songs in Rabindra Sangeet. He is the only poet to have created the national anthems of two nations. He wrote the national anthems for both India and Bangladesh—*Jana Gana Mana* and *Aamaar Sonnar Bangla* respectively. In the late 1920s, Tagore took an interest in painting and art. He also showcased his works in many successful exhibitions throughout Europe. He became India's leading contemporary artist. Tagore received the Nobel Prize for Literature in 1913, making him the first non-european to do so.

In 1883, Tagore got married to Mrinalini Devi and fathered five children. He died on 7th August, 1941, at the age of 80, at his ancestral home in Calcutta.

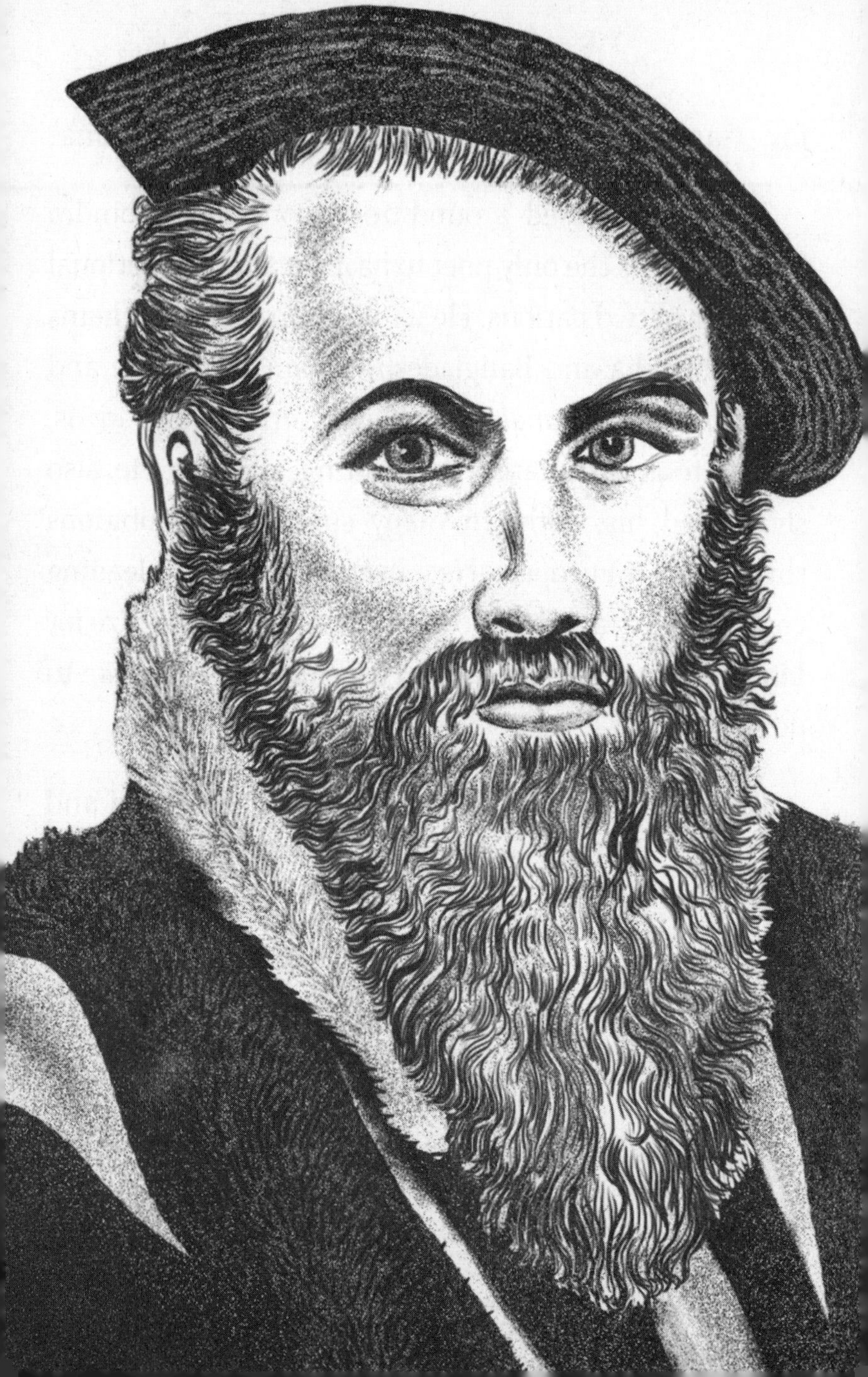

SIR THOMAS WYATT

BIRTH: 1503, Allington, England

DEATH: October 11, 1542 (aged 39)
Sherborne, England

Sir Thomas Wyatt was a sixteenth century English lyric poet, politician and ambassador. Wyatt introduced the forms of the Italian sonnet and the French short poem to English literature. His writing popularized Italian verse forms, most notably the sonnet, in England over half a century before Shakespeare.

Sir Thomas Wyatt was born in 1503, in Allington, England, to Henry Wyatt and Anne. He was the eldest son of the family. For his education, Thomas attended

St. John's College, Cambridge in 1515. He received his Bachelor of Arts degree in 1518 and his Master of Arts degree in 1522. After he graduated from college, Thomas became a member of Henry VIII's court circle. He was always famous and liked by many people because of his attractive appearance. Additionally, he was skilled in music, languages and arms.

Wyatt led an exceptional career. He served in diplomatic missions and was knighted in 1537. His fame rested mainly on his poetic achievements and his lyrics. His poems were unusual for their time. His writing showed a strong sense of individuality.

He developed new poetic forms—mainly, the sonnet. He introduced this form to the English court.

Wyatt was knighted in 1535. The next year, he was imprisoned in the Bell Tower for fighting with the Duke of Suffolk and also because he was rumored to be Anne Boleyn's lover, along with five others who were accused of the same. While Wyatt was held in the Bell Tower, he witnessed Anne Boleyn's execution. Disturbed by this event he wrote *V. Innocentia Veritas Viat Fides Circumdederunt me inimici mei.*

He released *Mine Own John Poins* in 1536-37. The poem was based on his own experience when he served his country. It was written in the form of an epistolary satire, one of three such poems. Wyatt praised country life and made sarcastic remarks about foreign governments in his writings. He became an ambassador for the court of the Holy Roman Emperor, Charles V in Spain. In June 1539, he returned to England. He again became an ambassador to Charles V in 1540.

He experimented in his own poetry with different Italian forms like the sonnet, ottava rima (stanzas of eight eleven-syllable lines) and terza rima (three line stanzas with a particular rhyme scheme). Wyatt wrote some of the first sonnets in the English language. Along with his contemporary Henry Howard, Wyatt was the most famous English poet of the mid-sixteenth century. Some of Wyatt's best lyrics and poems include *What No, Perdie!, Tagus, Farewell, Lux! My Fair Falcon, Forget*

Not Yet, and *Blame Not My Lute. Lux! My Fair Falcon* is believed to have been written in 1841 when he was imprisoned. The poem is sad in tone and expressive in its metaphors.

Wyatt was commonly recognized for introducing the sonnet to English literature. Wyatt's work was divided into two groups: the sonnets, poems, songs and lyric poems treating love, and satire. In 1557, more than ninety of his songs appeared in *Songs and Sonnets.* Some of the songs remained in manuscript, and it took many years for them to get printed. During the nineteenth and twentieth centuries, Wyatt's works were finally available in print.

Wyatt married Elizabeth Brooke in 1520. The couple had two children. They were in an unhappy relationship, and eventually separated.

Wyatt worked in many royal offices, but soon his health started to deteriorate. He died on 11th October, 1542 in England, after catching a fever.

Majority of his work was published after he died.

96 of his songs were published in 1557 in *Songes and Sonnets*. His work is generally divided into two groups: The first group includes the sonnets, rondeaus, songs and lyric poems, and the second group includes satires and psalms.

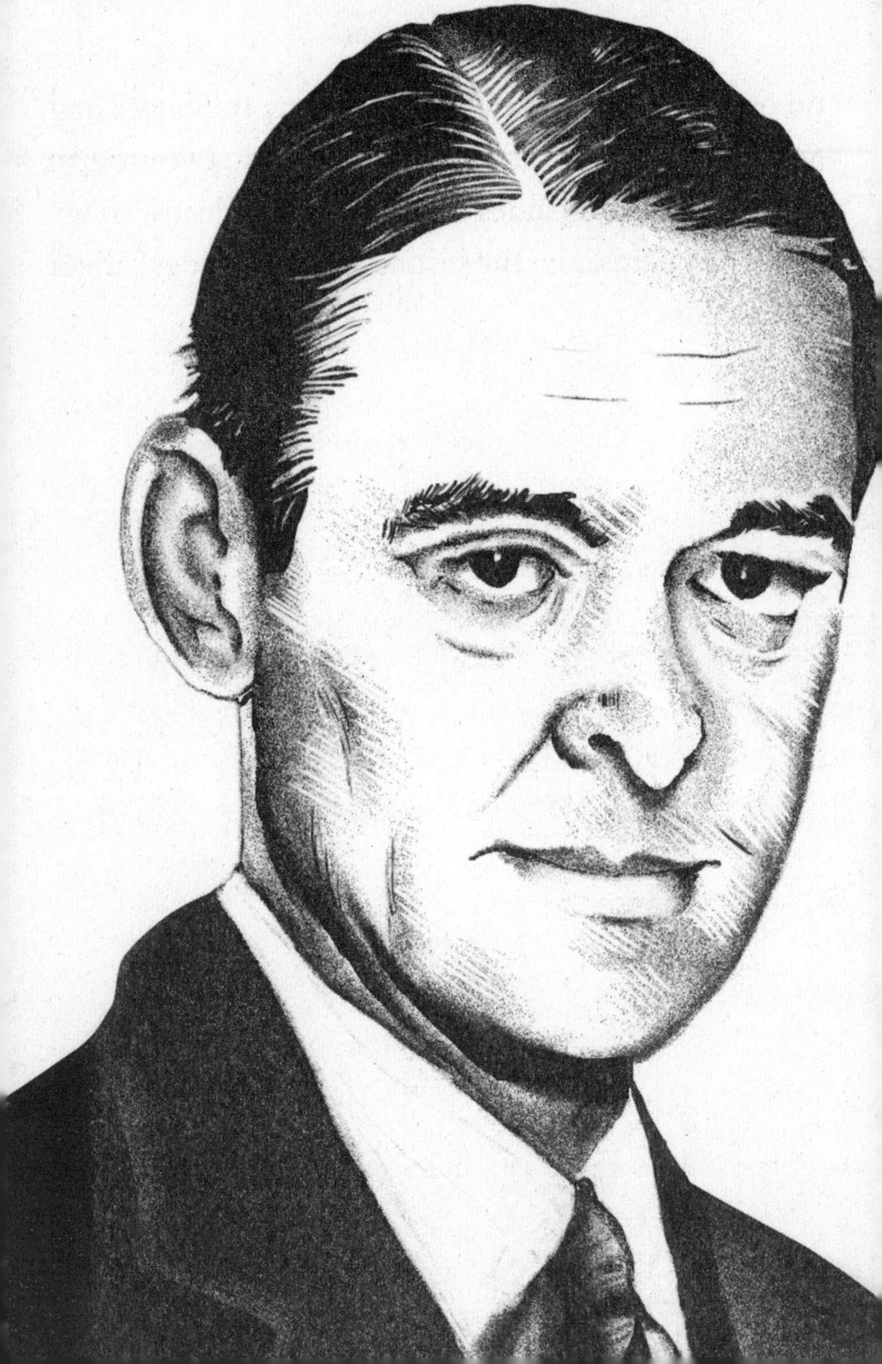

T. S. ELIOT

BIRTH: September 26, 1888
Saint Louis, Missouri, USA

DEATH: January 4, 1965 (aged 76)
London, England

T. S. Eliot was an American poet, literary critic, playwright and editor. He was a beacon of the Modernist movement in poetry.

Thomas Stearns Eliot was born in St. Louis on September 26, 1888, to Henry Ware and Charlotte Champ. Eliot had few friends as a child and spent most of his time reading. For his education, Eliot attended Smith Academy in St Louis. He learned different languages like Latin, Ancient Greek, French and German.

In 1905, he went to the Milton Academy in

Massachusetts. During this time, his literary talent started to bloom. He studied poetry through many great poets. Eliot eventually developed his own writing style. In 1911, he went to Harvard where he studied Indian philosophy and Sanskrit. World War I interrupted his studies and he transferred to Merton College, Oxford.

Eliot settled in London and met the famous American poet Ezra Pound. Pound helped Eliot publish his work upon recognizing his talent. In 1915, Eliot left Merton. He started teaching French and Latin at Highgate Junior School in London. He also wrote reviews.

Eliot's first poem was *The Love Song of J. Alfred Prufrock,* published in 1915. It was one of his most significant works throughout his career, and the first Modernist masterpiece in English literature. Eliot continued his studies even though he was busy with his job and writing career. He worked on his doctoral thesis for Harvard, which he completed in 1916.

In 1917, he received huge success following the

publication of his first book, *Prufrock and Other Observations*. The same year, he was offered a job at Lloyds Bank as a clerk. He accepted the job and worked there until 1925. While he worked in the bank, he wrote many poems and essays. Eliot also became editor of *Egoist*, a literary magazine, and worked for them till 1919. One of his most influential works published in the magazine was *Tradition and the Individual Talent*.

In 1919, he published *Poems*. One of the poems was called *Gerontion*. It was a blank-verse monologue which had no fixed lines. A poem like it had never before appeared in English literature. In 1920, he released *Sacred Wood*.

In 1921, he finished his first draft of *The Waste Land* and showed it to Pound. Pound edited many lines in his poetry. With his suggestions, the poem was completed as a 434-line poem. It was based on the period after World War I. It described the post-war generation's disillusionment and disenchantment; their wait for some form of redemption. *The Waste Land* was not Eliot's greatest literary poem, but it was his most famous work.

Eliot founded the journal *Criterion* in 1922. His poem *The Waste Land* was published in the first issue of the *Criterion*. In 1925, he left his bank job and joined Faber & Faber. Eliot continued as the editor of *Criterion* until it closed down in 1939. Eliot produced a few more notable poems including *Ash Wednesday*, a six-part poem in 1930, and *Four Quartets* published in 1943.

He even published many religious texts throughout his life. His lectures were published as *The Use of Poetry and the Use of Criticism*.

In 1936, he finished his collection *Poems 1909-1935* after writing *Burnt Norton*. Three more poems followed this poem, called *East Coker* (1940), *The Dry Salvages* (1941), and *Little Gidding* (1942). Together, these formed *The Four Quartets*. These poems were whole in themselves but were also interconnected.

Eliot's next major work was *Old Possum's Book of Practical Cats*, released in 1939. It was a book of the humorous poems for children that was later adapted into the hit Broadway musical *Cats*. The musical became one of the longest-running Broadway shows of all time.

Eliot received many honors in his life for his literary contributions. In 1948, Eliot was given the Nobel Prize in Literature for his outstanding contribution to modern poetry. In 1964, he received the Presidential Medal of Freedom. He was awarded three Tony Awards and thirteen honorary doctorates from established universities.

Eliot spent the last few years of his life in Europe. He died in London, England on January 4, 1965.

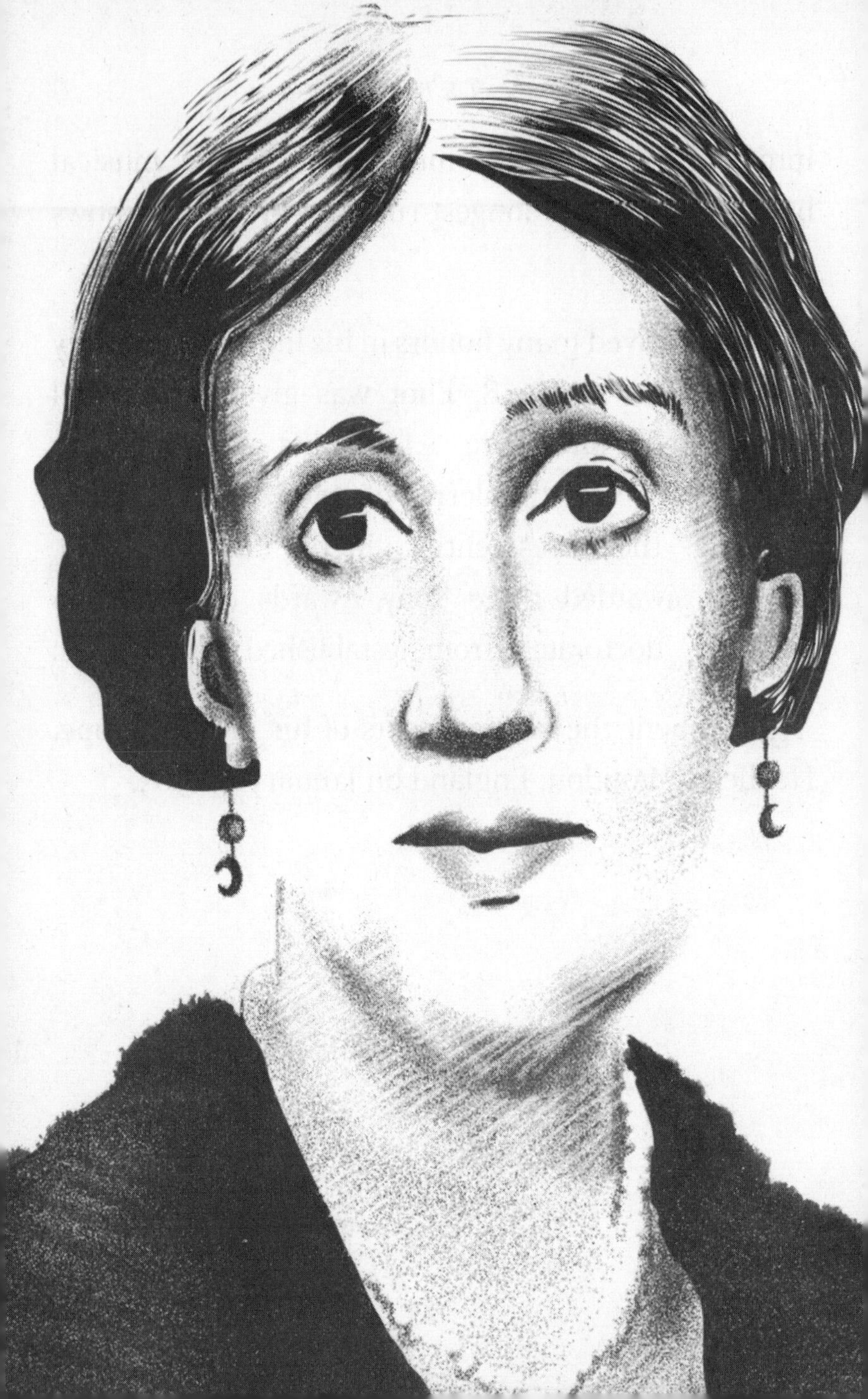

VIRGINIA WOOLF

BIRTH: *January 25, 1882,*
London, England

DEATH: *March 28, 1941 (aged 59),*
Rodmell, England

Virginia Woolf was an English author, essayist, publisher and critic. She was regarded as one of the leading Modernists and feminists of the twentieth century. Virginia was famous for her modernist classics. Her best works include *To the Lighthouse, Mrs. Dalloway, Orlando* and *A Room of One's Own.*

Virginia Woolf's real name was Virginia Stephen. She was born on January 25, 1882 in London, England, to Leslie Stephen and Julia Prinsep Jackson. Her father was an editor and a critic. Virginia was the third of four children. Her writing was shaped by the Victorian society, in which she grew up. She was home-schooled for most of her life and had her own library. She learned classics and English literature at home. In 1895, she spent most of her summer days in St Ives in Cornwall and made lots of fond memories. A place like St Ives inspired one of her masterpieces, *To the Lighthouse*. Virginia's mother died when she was only thirteen. She was devastated by her mother's death.

She started her literary career in the year 1900. Her first work was published anonymously. Eventually, she began writing for *The Times Literary Supplement*. Her writing career soon started to flourish. She met many great writers who formed the famous Bloomsbury Group. The group included well-known artists, writers and philosophers. She became an active member of this literary circle.

Over the next few years, Virginia worked on her first novel *The Voyage Out*, eventually published in 1915. The book's original title was *Melymbrosia*. The book was based on her own experiences. She kept on writing and self-published most of her work.

Together, Woolf and her husband founded the Hogarth Press to publish books. They published two short stories, Virginia's *The Mark on the Wall* and Leonard's *Three Jews*.

In 1919, Virginia published a novel titled *Night and Day*. Her third novel was called *Jacob's Room*, published in 1922. Woolf's fourth, and perhaps one of her most known novels was called *Mrs. Dalloway*. It was a feminist text set in post-first World War England. It is also a prime example of the 'stream of consciousness' form of narrative. This book was later adapted into a film.

The same year, she began another piece called *The Common Reader*. It was a collection of essays about English literature. And the next piece of writing was her world-renowned work of genius, *To the Lighthouse*.

Her 1928 novel, *To the Lighthouse* explored the theme of philosophical introspection; the plot was a secondary tool. The book contain-ed less dialogue and more observation. It also discussed the nature of art and perception. Following the success of this book, Woolf published her next novel, *Orlando* in 1928. The book follows an English nobleman who peculiarly turns into a woman at the age of thirty, and lives on for three centuries. Woolf received a lot of critical praise and popularity for this book.

In 1929, she went to women's colleges to deliver lectures. Her essays *A Room of One's Own* and *Three Guineas* were published next, exploring feminist themes and the concepts of fascism and war. Some of her essays discussed the hardships of women writers.

Another major work by Woolf was *The Waves*. It consisted of six characters, through whom Woolf explored the concepts of individuality and community. She published a novel called *Flush: A Biography* in 1933. The book captured a dog's stream of consciousness and viewed city-life from his eyes. Woolf published *The Years*, her final novel, in 1937.

Virginia married writer Leonard Woolf in 1912. They had a happy married life which lasted until her death. They founded the Hogarth Press together, which played a small part in her success as a writer.

Troubled by depression and other mental health issues through most of her adult life, Woolf committed suicide on 28th March, 1941, at the age of 59. Her novel *Between the Acts* was posthumously published as a tribute.

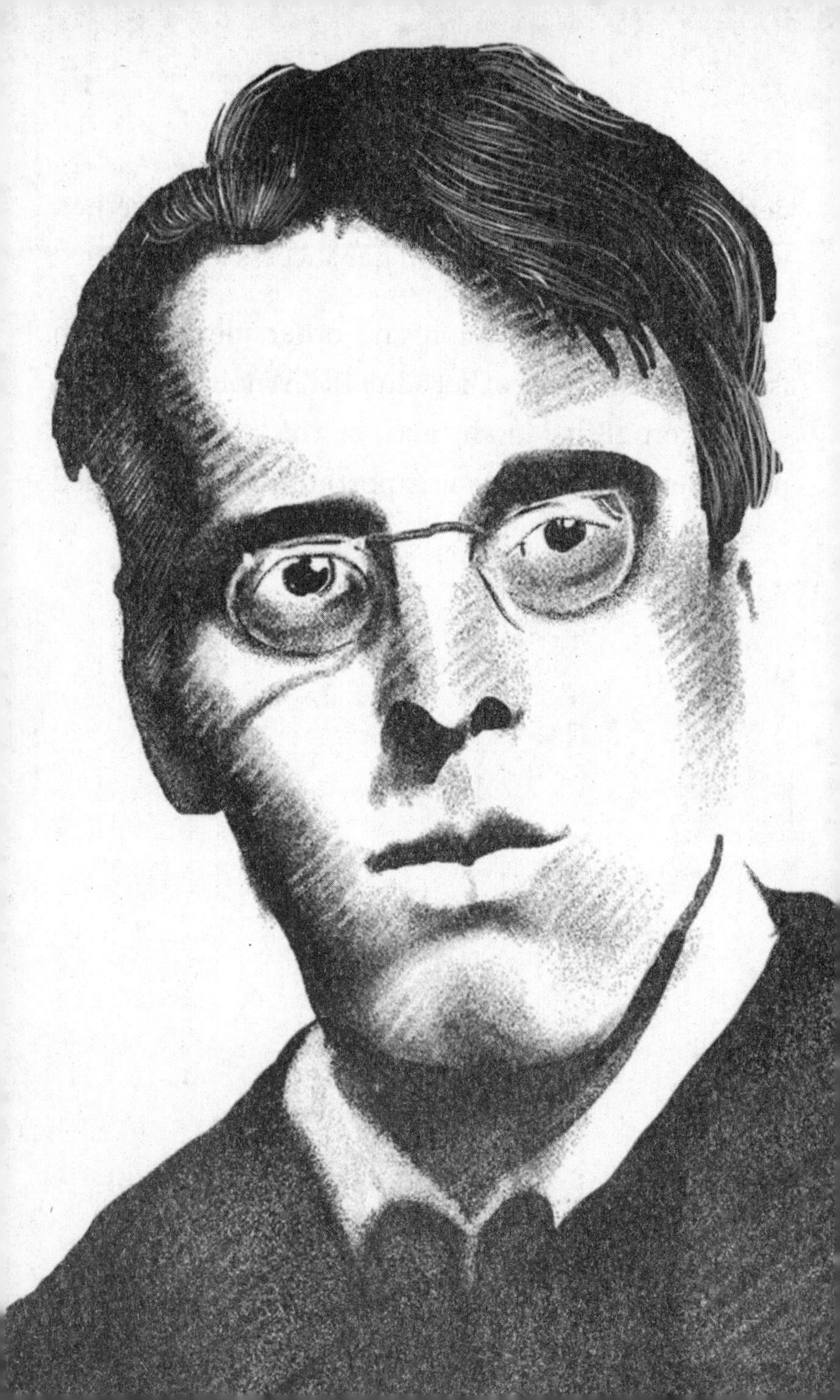

W. B. YEATS

BIRTH: *June 13, 1865*
Sandymount, Ireland

DEATH: *January 28, 1939 (aged 73)*
Roquebrune-Cap-Martin, France

W. B. Yeats was a famous Irish poet, dramatist and prose writer. Yeats made important contributions to both English and Irish literature. He was the first Irishman to get the Nobel Prize in literature.

William Butler Yeats was born on June 13, 1865 in Dublin, Ireland, to John Butler and Susan Pollexfen. His brother Jack Butler Yeats was a famous painter and Ireland's first Olympic medalist.

Being the son of a prominent portrait painter, he also took an interest in literature and poetry from a very young age. His writing contained a blend of aestheticism and atheism, based on the idea that there is no God. Yet, Yeats was always interested in magic and the supernatural. In 1867, his family moved to London when he was only two. But he lived with his grandparents. His family again moved to Dublin in 1880. There, he completed his high school education. Later, he went to the Metropolitan School of Art. In 1887, his family returned to London where Yeats decided to pursue writing as a career.

Two of Yeats' short lyrics were published in the *Dublin University Review* in 1885. Yeats also co-founded the Rhymers' Club along with English writer Ernest Rhys in 1890. The club released two collections of poetry between 1892 and 1894. It included many prominent London-based poets. He met Maud Gonne who was a supporter of Irish independence. She became a muse for him. He proposed marriage to her several times, but she turned him down every time. He dedicated his 1892 verse drama, *The Countess Cathleen*, to her.

Yeats joined the Golden Dawn, an organization that explored topics related to mysticism and the occult. In 1889, he published his first collection of poems called *The Wanderings of Oisin and Other Poems*. The title poem was about a mythic Irish hero. With this work, Yeats immediately caught the attention of the public.

His poems were highly inspired by Irish traditions and spiritualism. He had spent a lot of his childhood with his grandparents in Sligo, Ireland. The scenery and legends of the place where he grew up left a visible impact on his poetry. As a kid, he enjoyed reading the works of writers such as P.B. Shelley and William Blake.

Over the course of years, Yeats published numerous volumes of poetry. He published *Poems* in 1895. His poem *The Wind Among the Reeds* was inspired by folktales and legends. He published multiple collections of his works like *In the Seven Woods* in 1903, and *The Green Helmet* in 1910. From

1909, there was a fundamental change in Yeats' poetry. His next work *Responsibilities: Poems and a Play*, showed a new directness. He introduced the reality and its flaws with great imagination. In 1917, he wrote *The Swans at Coole*, followed by *The Tower* in 1928.

Yeats co-founded the Irish literary theater later called the Abbey Theatre in Dublin, in 1904 with Lady Gregory and others. He was the leading member of the Irish Literary Revival movement. Their primary focus was to create interest in Ireland's heritage and the growth of Irish nationalism. It became the flagship for young talent in the country. Yeats worked as a playwright for the theater. Some of his famous plays written during this time were *The Land of Heart's Desire* and *Cathleen Houlihan*.

Yeats got married to Georgie Hyde-Lees at a public registry office in 1917. The marriage was a happy one and they had two children.

Yeats was a devoted Irish Nationalist and in

1922 became a member of the new Irish Senate. He also served as a senator for six years till his retirement. Yeats became the first Irish writer to receive a Nobel Prize in literature in 1923. He died on January 28, 1939 in France, at the age of 74.

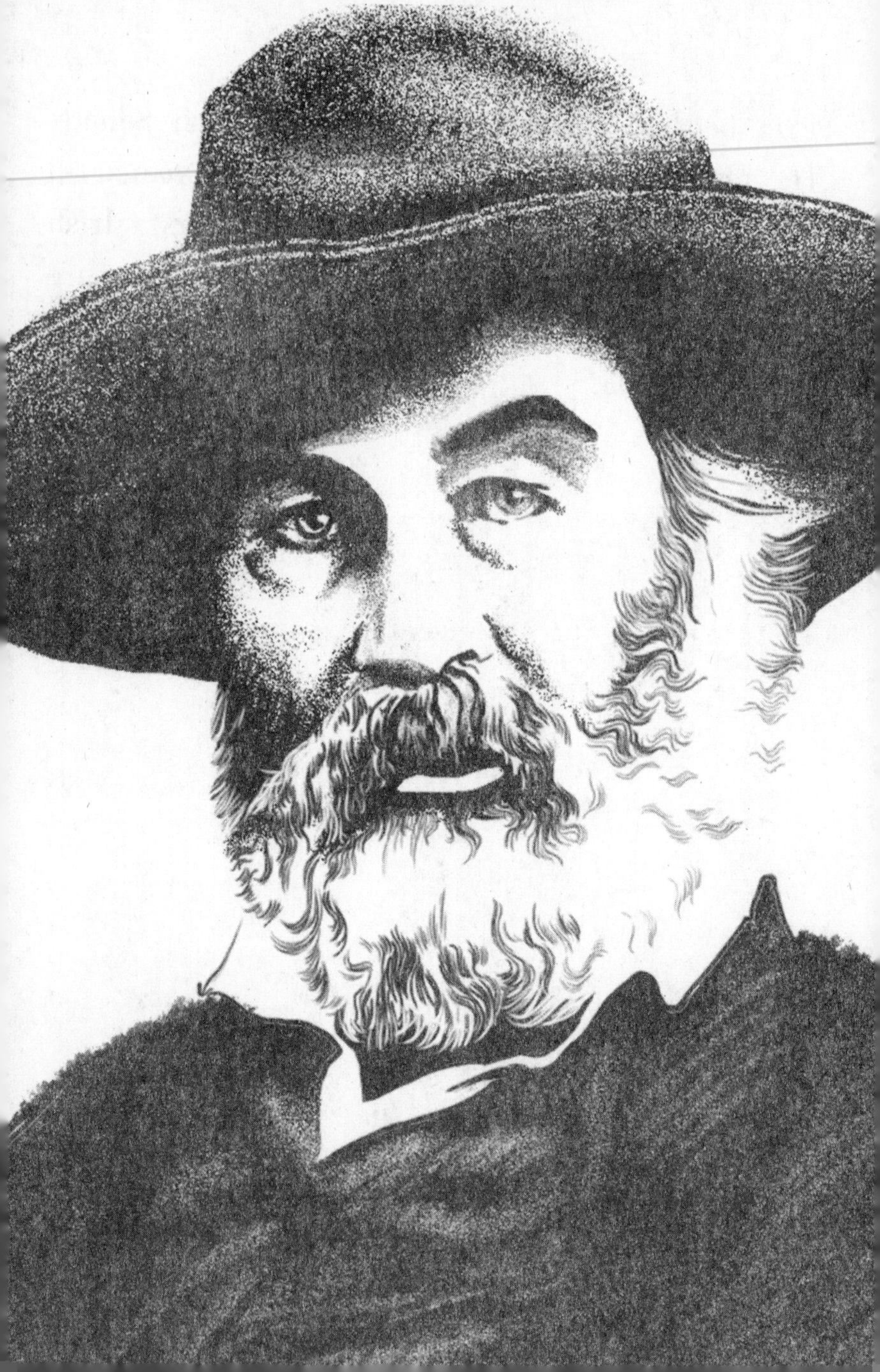

WALT WHITMAN

BIRTH: May 31, 1819
West Hills, New York, USA

DEATH: March 26, 1892 (aged 72)
Camden, New Jersey, USA

Walt Whitman was a great poet, journalist, essayist and humanist. His most famous works include his poetry collection, *Leaves of Grass*.

Walter Whitman was born in West Hills, New York, on May 31, 1819, to Walter and Louisa Van Velsor Whitman. His father was a laborer, carpenter and house-builder. His mother was a member of a religious group.

His family struggled financially and

Whitman's childhood was spent in poverty. Due to this, his family continuously relocated. Walt dropped out of school when he was eleven. He was mostly self-taught. He supported his family and worked as an office boy. Later, he got a job in the printing business where he learned the printing trade.

At the age of 23, Whitman became an editor at a daily newspaper in New York. He went on to edit many periodicals and newspapers. In 1846, he was hired as an editor of the *Brooklyn Daily Eagle,* a leading journal of the time. As an editor, he raised and supported controversial issues. Most of the time, his articles were rejected by his boss. Whitman changed jobs frequently but he never let his sense of liberty in his writing get compromised.

After having worked for so many newspapers, he went to New Orleans to try his luck. He worked at the *Crescent* as an editor. He realized the wickedness of slavery after he had worked there for only three months. Whitman came up with his own newspaper called the *Long Islander.* He served as the sole publisher, editor, pressman and distributor for ten months, after which he sold the publication to E. O. Crowell. He began to write poems instead, which he later published in *Leaves of Grass*.

In 1862, Whitman rushed to Virginia when he heard about the list of dead and wounded soldiers during the war. He feared that his brother George might be one of them. Thankfully, Whitman's brother had only sustained minor wounds during the American civil war. Whitman served as a nurse during the war, after he saw and felt for the vast number of injured soldiers in the hospital.

It was one of the most significant events in his life, which he mentions in his writings. He nursed more than thousands of patients and made hundreds of hospital visits during his part-time job. It exhausted him physically.

Walt Whitman wrote in free verse. The best-known proof of this is *Leaves of Grass*, a collection of twelve poems. He paid for its first publication initially and only printed 795 copies. The book received strong praise from the famous American essayist and poet, Ralph Waldo Emerson.

Whitman reworked this collection throughout his life. He revised it multiple times and by the time of his death, it had expanded to a collection of around 400 poems. It became one of the most famous works of American literature. It was praised for its clever use of free verse. Its style was also different from rigid poetic norms like rhyme and rhythm. Whitman's own life was reflected in the form of imagery and symbolism. The characters were based on his own personality.

Whitman's most famous poem was *Song of Myself*. The poem served as his autobiography. It is amongst the most famous poems written by an American poet. Whitman went on to write many well-known poems like *O Captain! My Captain!* This poem was about the death of American President Abraham Lincoln, who is described as the captain of the ship that is America. His poem *I Hear America Singing* expressed his love for America.

He was considered as a legendary figure, mainly due to his charm and his appealing personality. His face was described as "serene, proud, cheerful, grave". His features were massive and handsome with firm blue eyes.

He published his final poem *Good-Bye, My Fancy* in the final edition of *Leaves of Grass* in 1891. Whitman died on March 26, 1892, leaving behind a great legacy.

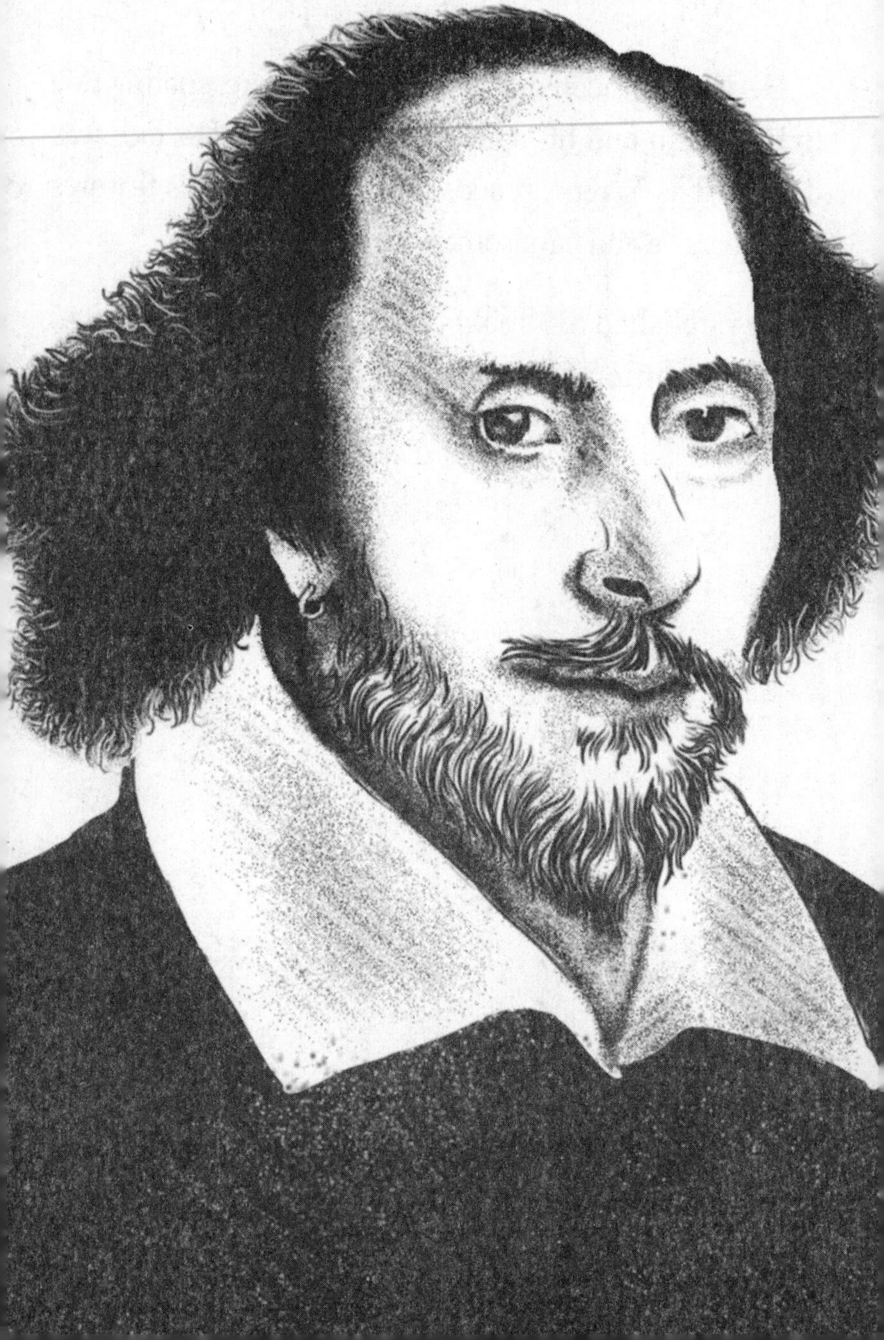

WILLIAM SHAKESPEARE

BIRTH: April, 1564
Stratford-upon-Avon, England

DEATH: April 23, 1616
Stratford-upon-Avon, England

William Shakespeare was the world's most celebrated English playwright, actor and poet. He was known as the 'Bard of Avon' and recognized as England's national poet.

William Shakespeare was born in April, 1564 in Stratford to John Shakespeare and Mary Arden. Shakespeare attended the Stratford grammar school. He was taught classics, Latin grammar, and literature. Shakespeare's life, before 1592, is completely undocumented. The time is known as the 'Lost Years'.

Shakespeare was a prolific writer. Around 1592, his plays started to get featured on the London stage. He even went on to act in many of his plays. Though, his work was first published post-humously by his friends in 1923, in a compilation called *First Folio*.

He was highly popular during the Romantic and Victorian period. George Bernard Shaw coined the term "Bardolatry", which referred to an extreme admiration for Shakespeare's works. Shakespeare, as a playwright and actor, grew by leaps and bounds. His name itself had become a strong selling point.

Shakespeare's most famous poems are his 154 sonnets. These sonnets were published around 1609. Shakespeare's short poems dealt mainly with the theme of lost love. His sonnets had a lasting charm due to his impressive writing and language skills.

Shakespeare used to write his plays based on historical accounts. His play *Hamlet* was based on the well-known legend of Amleth. Shakespeare's plays were separated into three main categories. First was comedy: popular works based on this theme are *All's well that Ends Well* and *Much Ado About Nothing*. The second was history which included *Henry V*. The third and final one was tragedy which included *Romeo and Juliet* and *Othello*.

His writing style was entirely different from other playwrights of the time. In his poetry, he used metaphors and expressive language. Later on, the writing became more traditional. Shakespeare captured the beauty of human emotions and conflict throughout his twenty years as a playwright. He treated his characters as human beings and not just fictional characters. Shakespeare's characters resonated with the audience. Compared to other playwrights' characters, who could come off a little flat, Shakespeare's characters were complex and human, and are relevant even today.

Some of his most notable works were *Hamlet, The Taming of the Shrew, Henry IV, Macbeth, A*

Midsummer Night's Dream, and *Julius Caesar,* he wrote a total of 37 plays in the early sixteenth century.

Shakespeare is often regarded as an Elizabethan playwright. After the death of Queen Elizabeth I, Shakespeare's company was awarded a Royal Patent by King James I.

Several Shakespearean plays were published and sold as popular literature. Shakespeare was known as an actor, writer and co-owner of the drama company Lord Chamberlain's Men, also known as the King's Men. Lord Chamberlain's Men performed most of Shakespeare's plays.

In his last few years as a writer, Shakespeare mixed tragedy and comedy and came up with tragic-comedies. Some of the notable tragic-comedy plays written by Shakespeare were *Cymbeline* and *The Winter's Tale.* Shakespeare's *The Tempest* written between 1610-11 was his last play.

Shakespeare married Anne Hathaway in 1582, at

the age of eighteen. They had three children. He died in 1616, at the age of 52.

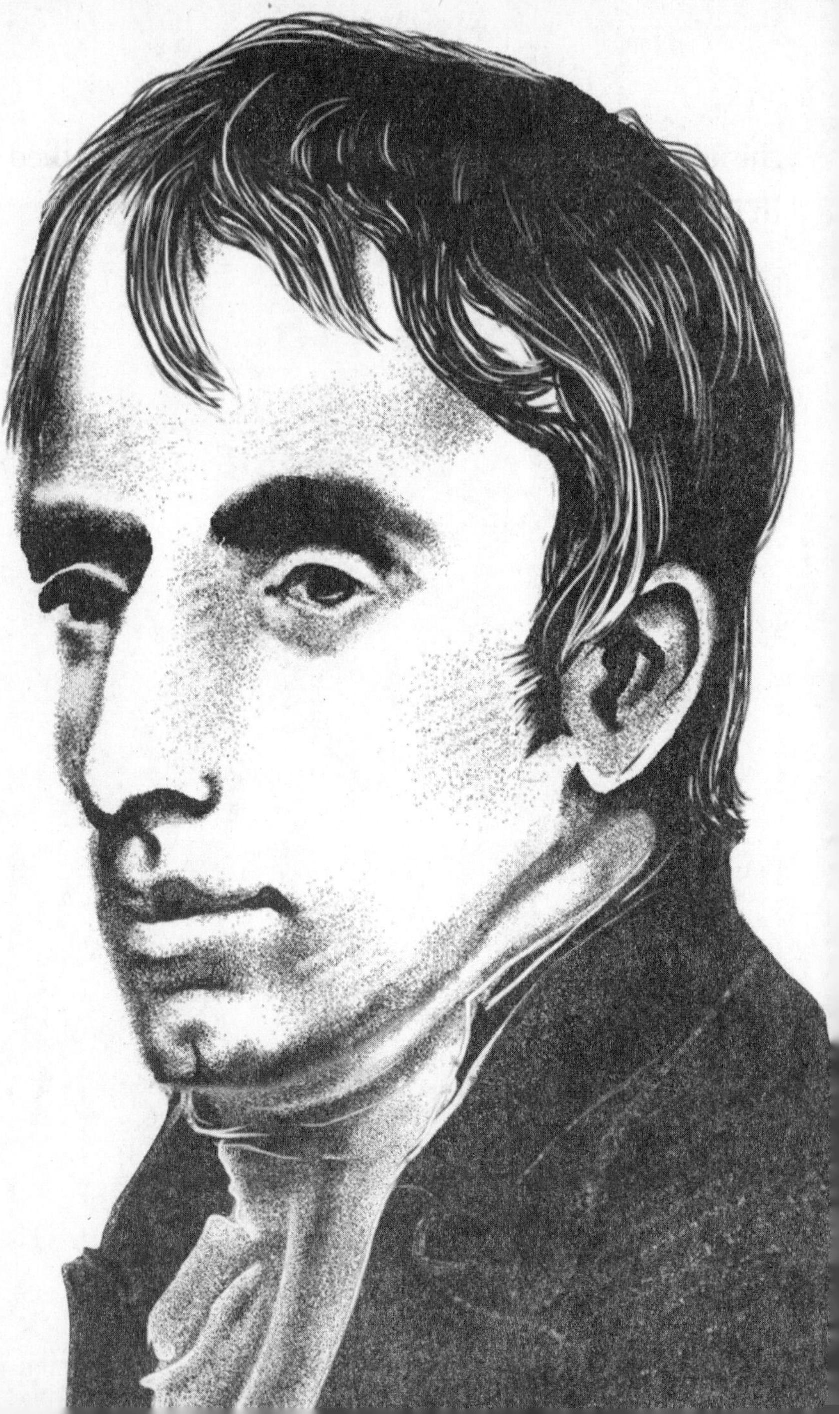

WILLIAM WORDSWORTH

BIRTH: April 7, 1770
Cockermouth, England

DEATH: April 23, 1850 (aged 80)
Westmorland, England

William Wordsworth was a famous English poet who played a significant role in the English Romantic movement. His best-known work was *Lyrical Ballads,* published in 1798. His love for nature influenced both his personality and his poetry.

William Wordsworth was born on April 7, 1770 in Cockermouth, England to John and Anne Wordsworth. He was the second of five children. His father was a legal agent. William was closest to his sister Dorothy. Wordsworth's mother died when he was just seven. He was sent to Hawkshead Grammar School after the death of his father. William moved to Cambridge University to continue his higher studies. During his time in Cambridge, he toured France and his experience profoundly impacted his interests in literature and poetry. The trip had an intense influence on his poetry. He graduated in 1790.

He released his poetry collections, *An Evening Walk and Descriptive Sketches* in 1793; they helped advance his career. In 1797, poet Samuel Taylor Coleridge reached out to Wordsworth. He collaborated with him and produced one of the most significant works of his career, *Lyrical Ballads* in 1798. It was a milestone for the English Romantic movement. He tried to use colloquial language in his poems. It caught the interest of ordinary people, and his readers felt connected to his writing.

In 1796, Wordsworth wrote his only play, which was turned down by the London theater. The play was called *The Borderers*, a tragedy set during King

Henry III's rule. At the peak of his career in 1807, he published *Poems in Two Volumes*. It was followed by *Guide to the Lakes* in 1810, *The Excursion* in 1814 and *Laodamia* in 1815.

Other works from his middle age include *The White Doe of Rylstone* and *Peter Bell*. The former is set in the backdrop of Elizabeth I's time, and is a story of a family that shatters during an unsuccessful rebellion against the Queen. *Peter Bell*, originally written in 1798, was re-written several times and finally published in 1819. In its later versions, it turned into an experiment in Romantic irony and mock heroism, colouring the poet's feelings with those of the hero.

Another most notable creation of Wordsworth's was *The Prelude*. This masterpiece was published posthumously in 1850. It was an autobiographical poem. *The Prelude* was written as an introduction to his long philosophical poem, *The Recluse,* which he never finished. The portions that he did finish were published as *Excursion*, in 1814.

Wordsworth published another famous poem, *Daffodils* in 1807. Wordsworth's sister, Dorothy was also a well-known poet and author. After the death of their mother, Wordsworth and his sister didn't see each other for a decade. They reunited in 1787 and became inseparable. Even though his sister was not famous like Wordsworth, her work was well-praised by critics. Dorothy played a crucial role in William's success.

Wordsworth toured France in his college days and met a French woman, Annette Vallon. He had a daughter with her, whom Wordsworth supported all his life. In 1802, he married Mary Hutchinson. The couple had five children. The death of his daughter Dora left him devastated.

Wordsworth received honorary degrees from Durham and Oxford. In 1842, he resigned from his government job and started to live on his pension. He spent the last few years of his life peacefully. He lived in a large house near Grasmere, England. The following year, he became England's Poet laureate (a famous poet as a member of the British Royal household).

He died on April 23, 1850 at his home in England at the age of eighty. Wordsworth not only created some of the most beautiful poetry of his times but also placed poetry at the center of human existence. He said that poetry for him was as immortal as the heart of man.

QUESTIONS

Q.1. *The Hound of Baskervilles* was published in which year?

Q.2. Who is referred to as the 'Father of the Italian language'?

Q.3. What was George Eliot's real name?

Q.4. Eric Arthur Blair was the real name of which author?

Q.5. What was *Pride and Prejudice*'s original title?

Q.6. Which famous writer is buried in the Mount Cemetery in Guildford?

Q.7. Which famous American writer was born in the small town of Florida, Missouri?

Q.8. What was the title of Oscar Wilde's last play?

Q.9. Tagore renounced his knighthood after which gruesome incident in history?

Q.10. Who is the world's most adapted and produced playwright?

Q.11. Who was known as the 'Queen of Crime'?

Q.12. T.S. Eliot won the Nobel Prize for literature in which year?

Q.13. Who was the writer of *Egoist*?

Q.14. What type of story was *A Farewell to Arms*?

Q.15. What are some of Charles Dickens' best books?

Q.16. What is the name of Arthur Conan Doyle's famous detective character?

Q.17. Who was awarded the Nobel Prize for Literature in 1954?

Q.18. Who was a significant figure in the Modernist movement during the twentieth century?

Q.19. What was the world's longest running play called?

Q.20. What was the name of the silent movie that was based on Charles Dickens' book?

Q.21. Who is the creator of the *Harry Potter* series?

Q.22. Sir Arthur Conan Doyle was part of which society?

Q.23. What was Dante Alighieri's famous work?

Q.24. What was the name of Mark Twain's most famous works?

Q.25. Name Walt Whitman's famous works.

Q.26. What was the name of J. K. Rowling's digital company?

Q.27. 'Rhymers' Club' was co-founded by whom?

Q.28.   What was the poem *Four Quartets* about and who wrote it?

Q.29.   Who was the first Irishman to get the Nobel Prize in literature?

DID YOU KNOW?

1. Agatha Christie loved archaeology which she also used in her writing.

2. Charles Dickens has appeared on the British ten-pound note.

3. In Italy, Dante has often been referred to as the 'Supreme Poet'.

4. Earnest Hemingway participated in the Spanish civil war and the invasion of France during World War II.

5. Ezra Pound's first published poem was a limerick, which appeared in his local paper when he was eleven years old.

6. George Bernard Shaw was a keen amateur photographer.

7. Agatha Christie drew many of her characters from real life, like her famous character Miss Marple, who was influenced by her grandmother.

8. The *Oxford English Dictionary* credits Eliot with the earliest known references to both "lawn tennis" and "pop" music.

9. George Orwell had a great interest in tea. He even published the essay *A Nice Cup of Tea* in the *Evening*

Standard.

10. The original *Harry Potter* manuscript was rejected by twelve publishing houses before Bloomsbury published it.

11. J.K. Rowling went from being unemployed to a millionaire in five years.

12. In just 25 years, John Keats published 54 poems, three novels and many articles.

13. Lewis Carroll suffered from a stutter most of his life.

14. Oscar Wilde wrote many plays and short stories, but he wrote only one novel, *The Picture of Dorian Gray.*